Huna

Ancient Hawaiian Secrets for Modern Living

Serge Kahili King, PhD

ATRIA BOOKS
New York London Toronto Sydney

BEYOND WORDS
Hillsboro, Oregon

ATRIA BOOKS

A Division of Simon & Schuster, Inc.
1230 Avenue of the Americas
New York, NY 10020

BEYOND WORDS

20827 N.W. Cornell Road, Suite 500
Hillsboro, Oregon 97124-9808
503-531-8700 / 503-531-8773 fax
www.beyondword.com

Managing editor: Lindsay S. Brown
Editor: Julie Steigerwaldt
Copyeditor: Jennifer Weaver-Neist
Proofreader: Marvin Moore
Design: Sara E. Blum
Composition: William H. Brunson Typography Services

First Atria Books/Beyond Words trade paperback edition November 2008

ATRIA BOOKS and colophon are trademarks of Simon & Schuster, Inc. Beyond Words Publishing is a division of Simon & Schuster, Inc.

For more information about special discounts for bulk purchases, please contact Simon & Schuster Special Sales at 1-800-456-6798 or business@simonandschuster.com.

Manufactured in the United States of America

10 9 8 7 6 5 4 3 2 1

Library of Congress Cataloging-in-Publication Data

King, Serge.
    Huna : ancient Hawaiian secrets for modern living / Serge Kahili King. —
1st Atria Books/Beyond Words.
        p.   cm.
    1. Huna.   I. Title.
    BF1623.H85K56   2008
    299'.9242—dc22

                                                    2008024323

    ISBN-13: 978-1-58270-201-8
    ISBN-10:   1-58270-201-2

The corporate mission of Beyond Words Publishing, Inc.: *Inspire to Integrity*

'Ike 'ia e ka nui manu
Recognized by many birds

To my workshop students from around the world,
who helped me to clarify and refine the ideas
presented in these pages

Contents

Acknowledgments

*S*pecial thanks are in order for my dear friend Alf Lüchow, who kept encouraging me to write this book; to my long-time friend and loyal agent, John White; and to my publisher, Cynthia Black, who, fortunately, likes my stuff.

Introduction

H una is a Hawaiian word meaning "secret," more in the sense of esoteric knowledge than a secret that cannot be shared. An alternate meaning is "very fine," like dust particles or sea spray. Rather than something to be locked away, it is simply hard to see or recognize. More details about it as an esoteric system will be revealed in the first chapter, so for now it is sufficient to know that the Hawaiian phrase *Ka Huna* translates as "The Secret," referring to the ancient wisdom of turning inner knowledge into outer success.

For more than thirty-five years I've been a practitioner of the Huna teachings and have dedicated myself to sharing that knowledge with the world. A word closely related and often associated with *huna* is *kahuna*, as in the American slang "big *kahuna*," or the top authority/boss. Because there is so much controversy and misunderstanding regarding this word, I'd like to clarify it here and how it relates to the study of *huna*.

First, a brief note about language conventions: in Hawaiian the plural for *kahuna* is *nākāhuna*. In English, however, adding an "s" to words indicates the plural, even in the case of foreign words (for example, *leis*, *luaus*, and *ukuleles*). So even though it is not correct Hawaiian, for ease of reading I will pluralize Hawaiian words by adding an "s." Also, Hawaiians speaking Hawaiian use the pronunciation "Hawai'i," but because I am writing in English, you'll notice throughout the book that I use "Hawaii," much like we say "Germany" instead of "Deutschland," "China" instead of "Zhōngguó," "Vienna" instead of "Wien," and so on. So I will use English conventions in writing most Hawaiian words. Now, let's get back to *kahunas*.

According to Lorrin Andrews, author of the first Hawaiian dictionary published in 1865, *kahuna* is a contraction of *kahu* ("to cook," especially in an earthen oven) and *'ana* (a particle that adds "ing" to a word). So the base meaning by this idea is "a cooking." This doesn't make much sense until you learn that *kahu* also means "to tend an oven, or to take care of the cooking." Ancient Hawaiian thought, from our point of view, was very symbolic or figurative, and a word for one type of activity or experience could be applied to other symbolically related activities or experiences. So *kahu*, originally referring to taking care of an oven, became a general word for taking care of anything. Another possible origin for the word *kahuna*, however, is that it is simply a combination of *kahu* ("to take care of") and *na* (a particle that makes words into nouns). In that case, a basic translation of *kahuna* would be "a caretaker."

Over time, languages change, and at some point *kahu* and *kahuna* both became nouns with somewhat different meanings. The word *kahu* came to refer not only to caretakers but to what are now known as "caregivers," as well as to administrators, regents, pastors, masters and mistresses of households, dog owners, and leaders of clubs, associations, orders, and other groups. The word *kahuna*, according to J. S. Emerson, an early observer of Hawaiian culture, "suggests more of the professional relation of the priest to the community."

Andrews defines a *kahuna* as "a general name applied to such persons as have a trade, an art, or who practice some profession," generally with a qualifying term added, such as *kahuna lapa'au*, a physician; *kahuna pule*, a priest; *kahuna kalai la'au*, a carpenter; *kahuna kālā*, a silversmith. Without any qualifying term, he notes, *kahuna* refers to the "priest or the person who offers sacrifices." Mary Kawena Pukui and Samuel H. Elbert, authors of the modern standard Hawaiian dictionary, define a *kahuna* as a "priest, sorcerer, magician, wizard, minister, expert in any profession (whether male or female)," adding that under the 1845 laws of the Hawaiian kingdom, doctors, surgeons, and dentists were called *kahuna* as well.

Samuel Kamakau, in *The People of Old*, mentions *kahuna* geologists, geomancers, psychics, martial artists, spear throwers, "and many other classes besides." In *Ruling Chiefs of Hawaii* Kamakau describes a *kahuna*, Paka'a, who was a master of geology, psychic perception, and navigation. He also describes many *kahuna* craftsmen who were chosen by King Kamehameha the Great to be in charge of dyeing; navigation; making canoes, surfboards, bowls; and many other crafts.

From this brief historical survey, and from reading these references in full, some things about *kahunas* are clear:

- They were the experts of old Hawaii—experts in religion, health, crafts, science, psychology, and magical practices of various kinds.
- *Kahuna* was a title, like MD or PhD, and additional descriptive words were used to designate the field of expertise.
- Just as the modern use of the word "doctor" by itself is generally taken to mean a medical doctor, so the use of *kahuna* by itself generally designated a priest or healer.

❖ *Kahunas* underwent intensive and extensive training before being recognized as experts in their field, either by their teacher or by the community.

❖ Some *kahunas* were experts in many fields.

❖ *Kahunas* could be male or female.

❖ Although it is not explicitly stated above, it is clear from reading the previously mentioned sources that *kahunas* of any kind in Hawaiian tradition were always attuned to the spiritual side of their expertise as well as to the material side.

❖ Under the monarchy the term *kahuna* eventually extended to foreigners who were recognized as experts in their fields, especially ministers and health professionals.

When Hawaii became a territory of the United States and a tourist destination, visitors discovered that the best surfer on the beach was called *kahuna nui he'e nalu*, the "principal master surfer." Because of his expertise he was also the leader among the surfers, and they would follow his advice on boards, waves, and the skill itself. He was called *kahuna nui* for short. This soon became the phrase "big *kahuna*," which took on meanings of "big boss" or even "the biggest and the best" in any area, including hamburgers.

In modern times the word *kahuna* is used and misused in many ways. Some people without any traditional Hawaiian knowledge or training claim to have been "initiated" as *kahunas*, something which Hawaiians of old would have laughed at or been shocked by. Some Hawaiians fear the word because they automatically relate it to sorcery, and some Hawaiians say that no one can be a *kahuna* who isn't a native Hawaiian. Some visitors come to Hawaii looking for a *kahuna* that is—to them— a psychic healer, while others come looking for a shaman.

Introduction

How do you know if someone is really a *kahuna*? There are no hard and fast rules, and there never have been. A deep knowledge and understanding of Hawaiian culture would seem to be a must if the word is to have any meaning in a Hawaiian context. In old Hawaii the main test would have been one's level of expertise in a given field of importance to Hawaiians. The teacher is the one who grants the title, so being able to name the teacher would seem to be a factor, too. So, what is a *kahuna*? Just a title that means what you think it does. If you meet a *kahuna*, respect the person for what he or she can do more than for the title. And if that person claims the title from a Hawaiian source, expect some knowledge of Hawaiian culture and esoteric wisdom, whether it is called Huna or something else, and some pride in naming his or her teacher.

Do you need a *kahuna* to learn or use Huna? Absolutely not. Huna is based on a set of ideas that can be applied to life situations by anyone. These ideas were part of ancient Hawaiian culture. A *kahuna* specializing in an area of life of interest to you might be able to help you, but just as you can learn how to run a business without going to college, so you can learn to use Huna without a *kahuna*.

I was trained in a traditional way in *kalakupua*, or *kupua* for short, a near equivalent to "shamanism," by my Auntie Laka and my Uncle Wana of the Kahili family, who originally came from Kauai. I was "hanai'ed" (a Hawaiian term for family-approved adoption) into that family as the grandson of Joseph Kahili in 1957. My last teacher, Wana Kahili, granted me the title of *kahuna kupua* in 1975 on Goleta Beach, California, based on the results of more than twenty years of training (including time with my father). Like most who have received a similar honor, I don't have a certificate to "prove" it and, since it was a private ceremony, there aren't any witnesses to attest to it. But I know what I know, and I know how to do what I do. That's enough for me. However, I don't use the title *kahuna* anymore. One aspect of Hawaiian culture I learned is to avoid offending others when you don't have to, and some Hawaiians are offended by my use of the title *kahuna*. So I am *Kahu* to members of my organization who want to call me by a title, "Dr. King" to those who want to acknowledge my doctorate in psychology, and simply "Serge" to the rest of the world. I have Hawaiian names as well, but I honor my birth parents by using the name they gave me, and I honor my Hawaiian family by using their name as my middle name in writing and teaching.

In addition to training with my father and with the Kahili family, I underwent a shaman apprenticeship in West Africa for nearly seven years with an African shaman. After returning to the States in 1971, I took up my *kupua* training with my Hawaiian uncle, and in 1973 I founded Huna International for the purpose of sharing this knowledge with the world. Under the name of Aloha International it has become a worldwide network of Huna healers, teachers, and students. And along the way I have written a dozen books, all related in some way to the Huna knowledge.

I think you will find that the applications of Huna provided in this book will be the most practical for the most purposes for the most people than any I have presented so far. My hope is that you can apply these techniques toward making your dreams come true, using the wisdom of Huna to strengthen your powers of mind, body, and spirit.

1

What Is Huna?

Hu'ea pau 'ia e ka wai
All scooped up by rushing water
(Everything is told, no secrets are kept)

O n the islands of the South Pacific, influenced by a world of sea and sand, volcanoes and palm trees, hurricanes and gentle breezes, there exists a unique path of living that is sometimes called "The Way of the Adventurer." It is an ancient path that is so powerful and so practical that it works as well in modern times as it did in the misty past. This way is based on a Polynesian philosophy called *Ka Huna*, which means "The Secret."

Before describing it in detail, however, it would be best to "talk story," as the Hawaiians say, in order to introduce the ideas that form the basis of Huna.

What Is New Is Old and
What Is Old Is Also New

It is 207 AD, and a middle-aged man, wearing a pure white robe made from the bark of a tree, squats down on an outcropping of lava rock facing the ocean. From out of a woven raffia pouch he takes a worn stone carved to resemble a fish and sets it down on the black lava. In a trilling, chanting voice, he speaks to the stone, moving it in various directions in response to some internal impulse that only he is aware of. Finally, he stops chanting, relaxes, and smiles down at the piece of stone that now points toward the mountains behind him. Then he stands up and shouts to the fishermen who have been waiting, "Get the nets ready! The fish will be here in abundance when the sun reaches kahiki-ku, (the sky overhead) in the late afternoon."

It is 2007, and a young woman in a well-tailored business suit is on her way to an important meeting. Strapped comfortably in the window seat of the 777 jet, she leafs through the airline magazine to pass the time. Suddenly she puts the magazine down, aware of an event forming in her environment. Moments later the plane shakes as it enters rough air, the warning lights for seat belts go on, and the captain's voice announces that everyone should stay seated because there will be considerable turbulence ahead. The woman calmly takes a deep breath and extends her spirit beyond the confines of the airplane. There she blends her energies with those of the wind, talks to it soothingly, and smoothes it out with her mind. Less than two minutes later all the turbulence is gone, so she lets go of the wind and returns to her magazine.

These two people, separated in time by almost two thousand years and living in radically different cultures, have something important in common: Both of them are practitioners of

Huna, and they have learned how to integrate its seven basic principles into their daily lives.

The First Principle:
The World Is What You Think It Is

To begin with, the man and woman in the example above have learned that the world quite naturally responds to their thoughts. Their personal experience is, in effect, an exact reflection of how they think it is—no more and no less than a dream. As Huna practitioners, they know that this dream we call physical reality is generated from beliefs, expectations, intentions, fears, emotions, and desires. In order to change the dream, they use Huna's first principle to shift "mindsets" at will in order to produce specific effects under various conditions.

The Second Principle: There Are No Limits

This Huna principle states simply that there really are no limits, no actual separations between beings. The ancient man was able to communicate with the stone, and through the stone with the fish out in the ocean. And the modern woman could leave her body in the seat to become one with the wind, and then go back again without the slightest difficulty. Believing that there are no limits is a way of granting oneself tremendous freedom, but its corollary is total responsibility for one's actions and reactions.

The Third Principle:
Energy Flows Where Attention Goes

In the third principle, energy flows where attention goes, a poetic way of saying that the concentration of attention on anything produces a concentration of energy connected with the object of focus, whether physical or not. And the energy thus concentrated will have a creative effect according to the nature of the thoughts that accompany the attention. The man on the lava rock face focused on the fish with the intent to influence their direction for the good of the community, and the woman on the plane focused on the wind with the intent to eliminate the turbulence for her comfort and that of her fellow passengers.

The Fourth Principle:
Now Is the Moment of Power

Both the man and the woman in the example operated with Huna's fourth principle, knowing that power exists only in the present moment. However, they also knew that this present moment is as large as their present focus of awareness. Their sense of time, then, is quite different from that of the typical modern person. Because one cannot act in the past or the future, one should not waste time on past regrets or future worries. At the same time, one can change both past and future in the present moment.

The Fifth Principle: To Love Is to Be Happy With

One of the most far-reaching and profound discoveries of those ancients who produced the Huna philosophy is that love is the greatest tool for effective action. The Hawaiian word for love is *aloha*, and the inner meaning is "to be happy with someone or something and to share this happiness." In this respect, love is both an attitude and an action. Love, then, is not only a feeling or a behavior but also a means for change. For the Huna practitioner, love is a spiritual power that increases as judgment and criticism decrease. A truly loving intent is the most powerful spiritual force the world can know. The Huna practitioner expresses love as blessing, praise, appreciation, and gratitude. Separation diminishes power and love diminishes separation, thereby increasing power. The ancient man connected with the fish through love, just as the modern woman connected with the wind.

The Sixth Principle:
All Power Comes from Within

The sixth principle teaches that all power actually comes from within. Neither the man nor the woman in the example called upon any force outside themselves to help them in their endeavors. Their power didn't come from their personality or from their individuality but from the common God-spark they know as the source of their own being. The power and energy of this source is infinite, already in touch with everything else, an integral part of Ultimate Source (or by whatever name one chooses to use for it). Since this source is within as much as without and there is never any separation from it, one has only to look inside for it.

The Seventh Principle:
Effectiveness Is the Measure of Truth

Being eminently practical, Huna practitioners of old developed this eminently practical principle that effectiveness is the only valid measure of truth. Absolute truth carried to its logical extreme comes out translated as "everything is." Since this is hardly helpful at the human level, the Huna practitioner measures truth by the question, "Does it work?" The practitioner therefore feels free to change mindsets, shift belief systems, and create or modify techniques in order to achieve the best effects in a given situation. Was it true that the ancient man really spoke with the stone and that it answered back? Yes, because the fish came. Was it true that the woman really blended with the wind and smoothed it out with her mind? Yes, because the turbulence stopped. Cause and effect are not the same for the Huna practitioner as they are for the ordinary person in modern society.

Huna is an ancient, pragmatic philosophy that grew out of an exceptionally keen observation of life by Polynesian *kahunas* of esoteric knowledge. In the Kahili family, this esoteric philosophy was passed down from earlier generations and codified into the seven fundamental ideas I have just shared. I first learned these ideas from my adoptive Hawaiian uncle in the form of specific Hawaiian words and associated proverbs. When it came time for me to share this wisdom with the modern world, I condensed the concepts into seven English phrases that, to me, represented the most practical aspects of each principle for modern students to begin their studies with. From the basis of these principles, the Huna practitioner learns quickly and effectively to view ordinary reality in extraordinary ways, to recognize extraordinary events in ordinary circumstances, and to create new circumstances at will. And life becomes an exciting adventure.

Did the Hawaiians Really Use Huna?

There has been some controversy as to whether the ancient Hawaiian practitioners ever used the word *huna* to describe their studies in esoteric knowledge. One non-Hawaiian writer on Hawaiian spirituality has even claimed that Huna was not a Hawaiian tradition and that the word was coined by Max Freedom Long, who wrote several books on Hawaiian esoteric thought in the 1940s and 1950s. So let's examine some local and non-regional sources to see what they can tell us about the word's origin.

First of all, regarding the notion that Max Freedom Long coined the word *huna*, Long based his research on the 1865 edition of *A Dictionary of the Hawaiian Language*, by Lorrin Andrews. In that dictionary we find *huna* defined as "to conceal, as knowledge or wisdom." Obviously, then, Max Freedom Long did not coin the word. He did declare, however, that this was the word that he would use to describe the system of Hawaiian esoteric (or secret) knowledge as he understood it. So, regardless of whether or not one agrees with Long's final version of Hawaiian esoteric knowledge, he clearly did not invent the word or its meaning.

But the question remains, did the Hawaiians themselves use the word *huna* to refer to their esoteric knowledge? This is not easy to determine from an oral tradition, but a few knowledgeable Hawaiians recorded details about their own traditions after the introduction of written language. Perhaps we may find some clues there.

Many of the ancient *heiau*, or temples, of Hawaii held a tall, wooden framework called *'anu'u* that was partially covered with *kapa*, or bark cloth, and which was used for offerings and as a place for priests to reveal the words of the gods. In announcing the revelation they would begin with the phrase "Let that which is unknown become known." In *'Ōlelo No'eau* (Wise sayings), a book of Hawaiian proverbs by respected Hawaiian scholar Mary Kawena Pukui, we find the same phrase in Hawaiian: *Ahuwale ka nane huna*. Pukui's own translation is "That which was a secret is no longer hidden."

Another reference to *huna* can be found in a nineteenth-century source: Samuel Kamakau, a knowledgeable Hawaiian writer in the 1800s, said, "In the old days in Hawaii, prophetic utterances and hidden sayings (*'ōlelo huna*, i.e., speech with secret meaning) were relied on."

In her book *Hawaiian Mythology*, Martha Beckwith relates ideas that shed light on the meaning of *huna*. According to her Hawaiian sources, twelve sacred islands once existed close to Hawaii in ancient times, with frequent communication among them. These islands were inhabited by spirit beings, but humans used to travel back and forth to them (a very shamanic concept). They are said to have been able to move under the sea, on the horizon, or into the air like a cloud, according to the spirit chief's will. After the great political and religious changes around the middle of the thirteenth century, these spirit islands were rarely seen.

One of the most famous of these spirit islands is called *Kanehunamoku*, usually translated as "The hidden island of Kane." (*Kane* in this sense was a kind of creator spirit.) A better translation may be "Land of the invisible creative spirit." In the *Hawaiian Dictionary*, by Mary Kawena Pukui and Samuel H. Elbert, the phrase *po'o huna* is translated as "mysterious, hidden, invisible, as the gods," so rendering "invisible Kane" as a valid translation. All of this is significant because there are many tales of *Kanehunamoku* in which humans travel there, learn esoteric knowledge (in other words, knowledge of arts and crafts unknown to humans before then), and return to share that knowledge with the rest of humanity.

In more modern times the beloved Edith Kanaka'ole, a famous *kumu hula*, or *hula* master, created this chant (my translation follows):

E Hō Mai
E hō mai ka 'ike mai luna mai e
*'O nā mea **huna** no'eau o nā mele e*
E hō mai, e hō mai, e hō mai e

Grant Us
Grant us knowledge from above

*The wise **secret** of the chants*
Grant us this, grant us this, grant us this

The Hawaiians of old typically did not give names to abstract concepts. For instance, while there are numerous words denoting specific forms of sexual behavior, there is no word for "sex" or for "sexuality" as a concept. The closest one could come to that in Hawaiian, without inventing a new word, would be *ka mea ai*, which translates as "the coition thing." Likewise, there is no one overall term in Hawaiian for metaphysics or esotericism. "Huna," my Hawaiian uncle told me, "is just a nickname for *ka 'ike huna*, the hidden knowledge, or *ka 'ike pō*, the knowledge of the inner world. We use it because it's easier in English to give that knowledge a nice, short name."

There can be no doubt that the Hawaiians had a system of esoteric knowledge and practice, as these few references indicate. It is also evident that they used the word *huna* to refer to this knowledge in many ways. That they called this body of knowledge Huna is undoubtedly not so. Max Freedom Long found it convenient and so did my Hawaiian family. I know of other Hawaiian families who also used the word "Huna," while others use different terms today for describing it. The names are arbitrary; the knowledge is real.

The Seven Principles in Proverbs

There is no doubt that *ka 'ike huna*, the esoteric knowledge of using the power of the mind to influence nature and events, was practiced by the Hawaiians. References to it abound in written records. But did they practice what we now call the Seven Principles of Huna?

A great deal of information about a culture's philosophy can be obtained from looking at its proverbs, and we find many examples of the principles in practice among Hawaiian proverbs collected by researchers. Here are seven proverbs related to the seven principles, in their respective order, from Mary Kawena Pukui's book *ʻŌlelo Noʻeau*.

1. ***ʻAʻohe pau ka ʻike i ka hālau hoʻokahi*** **("All knowledge is not taught in one school"):** A variation on the idea that there are many sources of knowledge and many ways to think about things. The word *hālau* is actually a long, open-sided shed that was once used for storing canoes or as a meeting place for different kinds of activities, especially teaching. In its extended use, it also referred to the group that met there. Today it is almost exclusively used to refer to *hula* troupes. Even with something as important to the culture as *hula*, there were many masters and many schools, each with their own traditions and practices. *Corresponding Huna principle: The world is what you think it is.*

2. ***ʻAʻohe puʻu kiʻekiʻe ke hoʻāʻo ʻia e piʻi*** **("No hill is too high to be climbed"):** A way of saying that nothing is impossible. *Corresponding Huna principle: There are no limits.*

3. ***He makau hala ʻole*** **("A fishhook that never fails to catch"):** Said of one who always gets what one wants. The fishhook was a primary symbol of concentrated attention, and a good fishhook was said to be able to attract fish even without bait. This is because of the pervasive idea that a focused intention has what we might call today "a magnetic attraction." *Corresponding Huna principle: Energy flows where attention goes.*

4. ***Wela ka hao!*** **("Do it now!"):** Literally, "Strike while the iron is hot!" This is a clear message that the power to act is in the present moment. It is interesting to note that this

concept is based on how the Hawaiian language is constructed. Having no past or future tenses and no verb "to be," ancient Hawaiian thought related everything, including memories and expectations, to the present moment. So a phrase like "I went to Maui last week" would have been translated as "My having gone to Maui last week is over right now." And "I will go to Kauai next week" would have been "My going to Kauai next week hasn't happened yet." Such a concept leaves no time for guilt or worry and is a perfect example of the Hawaiians' ability, even today, to live in the present moment. *Corresponding Huna principle: Now is the moment of power.*

5. *He 'olina leo ka ke aloha* (**"Joy is in the voice of love"**): The word aloha is commonly used as a greeting in Hawaii, but what it really means is "love." Unlike Western concepts of love, however, *aloha* has no negative connotations whatsoever. The test of love, Hawaiian-style, is how kind you are and how happy you are. *Corresponding Huna principle: To love is to be happy with.*

6. *Aia no i ka mea e mele ana* (**"Let the singer select the song"**): A poetic way of acknowledging that real power comes from within. At every level of ancient Hawaiian society, one's authority in any area was directly related to one's ability to demonstrate the required skill involved. Even a high chief like Kamehameha the Great had to prove himself when he landed on one of his domains by being able to dodge spears thrown by local warriors. The ancient Hawaiians did not acknowledge inherited power alone, nor did they engage in empty rituals of initiation. An individual must realize his or her own power. *Corresponding Huna principle: All power must come from within.*

7. *'Ike 'ia no ka loea i ka hokua o ka 'ale* (**"Show your knowledge of surfing on the back of a wave"**): As

Hawaiian expert Mary Kawena Pukui put it, "Talking about one's knowledge and skill is not enough. Let it be proven." Although related to the meaning of the previous proverb, this concept is what enabled the Hawaiians to quickly adopt and adapt anything useful that came their way. To mention just a few examples, they turned hymns into a rich musical tradition, a Portuguese guitar into the *ukulele*, and the cattle-herding skills learned from Spanish *vaqueros* into the world-renowned subculture of the Hawaiian cowboy, or *paniolo*. *Corresponding Huna principle: Effectiveness is the measure of truth.*

The Ethics of Huna

From time to time people ask me about the ethical side of Huna because at first glance the seven principles seem to be amoral. That is, some people are bothered by the principles' apparent lack of any clear guidelines for behavior—no shoulds or oughts.

However, as is appropriate for "hidden knowledge," the ethics are implicit in the principles. If you use them logically, you can't help but be ethical. Let's examine them one by one in that light.

1. *The World Is What You Think It Is*

If you accept that the world is what you think it is, consciously and unconsciously, then it only makes sense to work on changing your beliefs for the better in order to have a better life. After all, we are really talking about your subjective experience of the world, not some imagined objective world. Like it or not, subjective reality is all you're going to get. A fascinating implication of this is that your subjective experience itself will clearly tell you how well you are doing in the thinking department. Life will be good to the degree that your thinking is good. You can't hide from your beliefs.

2. *There Are No Limits*

If there are no limits, then the Universe is infinite. Some scientists like to speculate about multiple universes and even multiple infinities, but they are just playing with words. "Universe" means the whole thing, and "infinite" means, well, infinite. The idea of an infinite universe implies that all of it is everywhere and every*when*, which then implies that every part of it is infinite. And that implies that you are, too. Which, finally, implies that you are always encountering yourself, in some guise or another. So it makes sense to be kind to your neighbor because your neighbor is yourself.

3. *Energy Flows Where Attention Goes*

If energy flows where attention goes, then sustained attention—conscious or unconscious—gives power to the object of attention. Dwell on sickness, and sickness will increase in your life; dwell on happiness, and you will have more of it; focus on lack, and the lack will be more evident; focus on abundance, and abundance will abound. Of course, if your focus is mixed, you will get mixed results. It pays to pay attention to your attention.

4. *Now Is the Moment of Power*

If now really is the moment of power, then every moment is an opportunity to change your life for the better. In any moment unfettered by past or future considerations, change can happen instantaneously. The most interesting thing about this concept is that when the mind or the body has such an opportunity, it automatically moves toward peace and happiness—as if ethics were already built in. For example, when your mind is fully in the present moment and free of any thoughts of past or present, you enter into a state of calm confidence; when your body is in that same state, the lack of emotional tension allows your natural healing processes to speed up considerably; and when two people meet without any past issues or future fears, they immediately become friends.

5. *To Love Is to Be Happy With*

If you define love as the behavior of being happy with someone or something, then increasing your loving is a practical thing to do. The ancient wise ones who developed these ideas noted the curious fact that happiness increases as happiness increases, meaning that you have to spread it around to keep it going. This kind of happiness does not imply a giddy, carefree, positive, band-aid kind of happiness. The word *aloha* (or love), from which the principle is derived, also includes the concepts of mercy, compassion, grace, charity, and all of the other good things that come under the name of love (it does not include any of the negative things). As you practice love, you increase love and happiness for all concerned.

6. *All Power Comes from Within*

If all power comes from within, then everything has the same source of power—an idea that logically follows from the second principle, "There are no limits." The difference lies in the manner and skill with which it is applied. However, there is a frequently overlooked aspect of power that is important to keep in mind: True power comes from the ability to empower. Hydroelectric power comes from using the power of falling water to empower machines to generate electricity. Political power comes from using the power of a society to empower individuals to give orders or pass legislation. Power has no single beginning or ending or source; it keeps changing focus. As more people become aware of their power to empower, it becomes natural for them to give it more careful consideration and use it for the good of all concerned.

7. Effectiveness Is the Measure of Truth

If effectiveness is used as the measure of truth, then the feedback from our experience will easily guide us toward more effective behavior. We learn to walk by ignoring our mistakes and repeating our successes. In fact, we learn most of our skills and behaviors not by trial and error, as is generally assumed, but by trial and repetition of what works. This idea of effectiveness is based on the Hawaiian word *pono*, a concept of goodness, rightness, or appropriateness. In ancient culture it meant the greatest good for the greatest number, not as defined by some arbitrary rules but by the actual experience of success, prosperity, health, and happiness. In this sense, then, the truth of your actions will be demonstrated by the results as they are experienced by all involved.

In the history of ethics, according to *Funk and Wagnalls Encyclopedia*, "There are three principal standards of conduct, each of which has been proposed as the highest good: happiness or pleasure; duty, virtue, or obligation; and perfection, the fullest harmonious development of human potential." The ethics of Huna include all three in the practice of the seven principles as outlined above.

2

Turning Dreams into Deeds

'Eu kōlea i kona puapua; 'eu ke kanaka i kona hanu
A plover moves by means of its tail;
a man moves by means of his breath
(Your power to act comes from yourself)

The Seven Principles Today

Huna wisdom may be applied to anything, but it is particularly well suited to accomplishing goals, achieving success, and turning dreams into deeds. In this chapter we'll look at how the seven principles of Huna can guide us toward success. We'll discuss the role that personal power plays in achieving our goals and study a practical program to begin each day in alignment with these goals.

First I'd like to share the Hawaiian word for each of the seven Huna principles and then an associated proverb often used by my Hawaiian uncle and teacher, Wana Kahili. Each principle has a direct application to achieving success.

1. *The World Is What You Think It Is*

'Ike means "to see, know, feel, perceive, be aware, understand," and in its active form of *ho'ike* it means "to show, demonstrate, explain, reveal, experience." The general idea in the philosophy is that our way of seeing the world determines our experience of the world. My uncle liked to say, *Mamua ka 'ike, mahope ka 'ike* ("First we perceive, then we experience"), using a play on two meanings of the word.

Fundamental to Huna is the idea that the skillful use of one's mind is an immensely powerful way to influence one's physical and emotional behavior. And it is that behavior, after all, that determines personal experience of the world. By relating our behavior to our thinking we can discover the mental patterns that mold our habits, and by consciously changing our thinking we can change our habits. These new patterns of behavior will evoke new responses from the world around us; there is no separation between ourselves, our environment, and the other people in it. Those who realize these truths achieve remarkable feats indeed, such as Kamehameha the Great, who united the Hawaiian Islands into a single kingdom recognized by all the major world powers of his time.

2. *There Are No Limits*

Kala means "to loosen, untie, free, release, forgive." The main idea is that all limits are arbitrary and the Universe itself is infinite. My uncle liked to say, *Ana 'ole, ka pō, 'ke ao* ("The inner world and the outer world have no limits"). In practical terms, this is saying that if the Universe is infinite, then anything is possible if you can figure out how to do it. Everything you do influences the world around you.

The modern concern with ecology is based on the idea that everything is interconnected and that you can't change anything in isolation. Whatever you do will affect something else, and changes around you will also affect you. It is increasingly accepted that we can't cut down all the trees, continue to dump our wastes into the ocean, or keep sending pollutants into the air without serious consequences for all the life on this planet. Meteorologists carry on this idea when they say, following chaos theory, that a butterfly fluttering its wings in Japan can cause a thunderstorm in the Rocky Mountains. Personally, we are used to the idea that the state of our environment and of our body can affect our mind. But many people are still coming to terms with the idea that our state of mind can affect our body and even our environment. Limits and boundaries exist in our perception but not necessarily in our experience. King Kalākaua, the last king of Hawaii, had this idea in mind when he became the first monarch in history to circumnavigate the globe.

3. *Energy Flows Where Attention Goes*

Mākia means "aim, purpose, to aim or strive for, to concentrate on." My uncle said, *Mākia ke ali'i, ehu ka ukali* ("Concentration is the chief, activity is the follower").

Have you ever noticed that the more interested you are in something, the more likely you are to do something about it? You might buy a book that got a great review, see a movie highly recommended by a friend, even change your lifestyle to please a new boyfriend or girlfriend. Whatever holds your interest will also tend to attract your emotional and physical energy. On the other hand, have you also noticed how the things you lose interest in fade into the background of your life along with the things that never interested you in the first place?

The more successful a person is, the more they direct and hold their attention on something by conscious choice. They don't just wait for something to catch their attention; they go out and catch something with their attention. When you learn to focus your attention at will and hold it on something for as long as you choose, you will have gained one of the most profoundly effective skills a human being can attain. Hawaiian legend Duke Kahanamoku kept his focus and won three gold and two silver medals for swimming in the Olympics of 1912, 1920, and 1924. He introduced surfing as a sport to the world, became the first person inducted into the Swimming Hall of Fame and the Surfing Hall of Fame, and served thirteen consecutive terms as sheriff of Honolulu.

4. *Now Is the Moment of Power*

Manawa means "time, season, affections, feelings." "Now is the moment of power" is a direct translation of my uncle's version: *Noho ka mana i keia manawa.*

You have to admit that neither the past nor the future have any power because you can't touch them, taste them, feel them, see them, smell them, or react to them in any way. For all practical purposes they don't even exist.

"What's that?" you cry. "What about all the things, good and bad, that shaped my life? What about the skills I learned, and the pain I endured, and all my experiences? And what about all the things that are going to happen that we have to prepare for? How can you say they don't exist?"

Ah, but all you have right now are the memories of all those things—the skills, pains, and experiences. And it's the memories you respond to now, not the past itself. The memories exist in the present moment, and you can alter your relationship to them—change your thinking about them—and thereby change their effect on your life. As for the future, no one—not the best psychic or the best-equipped meteorologist—knows what is going to happen ahead of time. People can make logical or intuitive guesses, sometimes proving to be right and sometimes proving to be wrong, but no one truly knows.

It really boils down to our personal opinions and practicality. If you think of the past as unchangeable and having the ability to exert power on the present, then it's easy to fall into a victim consciousness and not exert any effort to change. But if you think of the past as over and powerless, you can give yourself the freedom to make any changes you want to. Likewise, if you think of the future as fixed or predestined, then there is little incentive to take charge of your own life. And if you accept some combination of predestination and free will, then you will use your free will in those areas where you think you have it, and you won't use it in those areas where you think you don't.

Think of the future as a blank slate and you can give yourself permission to try anything. Ka'ahumanu, the youngest and favorite wife of Kamehameha the Great, gave herself this permission when the old king died. Following tradition, Kamehameha named his eldest son, Liholiho, as heir to the kingdom. Unfazed, Ka'ahumanu entered the king's hut alone just before he died, and when she came out she announced that the king's dying wish was to name her as Queen Regent to the throne (something like a prime minister). Such was her presence that she maintained her control of the kingdom with no opposition from 1819 to 1832 and even named Kinau, a daughter of another wife of Kamehameha I, as her successor.

5. *To Love Is to Be Happy With*

Aloha means "love, affection, compassion, sympathy, kindness, charity," and so much more. My translation of the fifth principle is based on my uncle's use of a special way to form a proverb: *Ke aloha, ke alo, ke oha, ka hā*—"Love (*aloha*) is being in the presence of someone or something (*alo*), sharing joy (*oha*), sharing life (*hā*)." The actual phrasing of the statement, though, comes from Barry Kaufman's book (of the same name) about using the concept with autistic children.

Love includes the active states of kindness, desire, enthusiasm, passion, and excitement, as well as the passive states of happiness, compassion, friendship, caring, and mercy. Whether active or passive, the motivation of love induces action that changes or influences things, and that is the essence of power. You could say that love is both electric and magnetic, seeking and attracting. It is the driving force that causes things to happen—the gentle energy that melts away resistance. It was this kind of love that caused the last queen of Hawaii, Lili'uokalani, to abdicate her throne under protest in 1893—rather than allow the shedding of blood—when an armed force, backed by the U.S. military, took over the government.

6. *All Power Comes from Within*

Mana means "supernatural or divine power, miraculous power, authority, power." My uncle taught that *Mai ka pō mai ka mana* ("Power comes from the inner world"), referring to the infinite source shared by everyone and everything.

This concept tells us that there is no power outside of us—no person, being, object, or circumstance that has any power over us. By our own decision and belief we can act like others have more power over our life than we do, but the power to do that also comes from within. God (or whatever name you prefer) doesn't act upon us but through us. According to this principle, if you have a dream, you have the power to make it come true. Of course, you also have the power to make it difficult. Hawaiian legends abound with tales about men and women, with seemingly little outward power, who used their inner power to overcome tremendous odds to win success for themselves and their loved ones.

7. *Effectiveness Is the Measure of Truth*

Pono, the word representing the last principle, means "goodness, moral qualities, correct or proper procedure, excellence, well-being, prosperity, success, assets, use, purpose." My translation follows my uncle's proverb, *Ana 'oia i ka hopena* ("Truth is measured by results").

Would you call a man successful who had reached the top of his profession and had ruined his health in doing it? Could a woman be called successful after raising a healthy, happy family if she ended up depressed and unfulfilled? If you gain the world but lose your soul, is that success? If we measure success by results, and if there are no limits, then the results we measure must include not only the achievement of goals but the consequences of achieving those goals. In other words, we must consider the personal, social, and environmental aspects of any endeavor to determine how successful it is. Following the Huna philosophy, harmony in those three areas is more important than balance. So whether you are striving for riches or recognition, intimacy or friendship, health or fitness, take a look at how your striving is affecting you personally, the people around you, and the world around them. When the results are good, they are *pono*. The famous Hawaiian culture hero, Maui, also known today as the "Hawaiian Superman," loved adventure for the sake of adventure but always shared the benefits of his adventures with the rest of humanity. He is traditionally associated with sharing the secrets of fire, agriculture, and many kinds of crafts.

Power and Purpose

Huna philosophy and personal power are inextricably connected, so let's take a closer look at that important concept. A better understanding of power will enable you to use it in the most effective way and with the most purpose behind it.

The essence of power is influence. Influence enables you to be effective at doing what you want to do, to get the intended results, and to move others to help you. Influence affects others' power even when it is unintentional.

Everything has both active and passive aspects of power. A flower has the active power to grow, blossom, and reproduce. It may also have the passive power to give food to a bee or pleasure to a human, both of which enhance its active power to grow and reproduce. You may have the active power to perform a certain task. You may also have the passive power to inspire other people by that performance.

There are several kinds of power:

1. The power of energy (as of the elements, strength, emotions, vibrations)
2. The power of favor (as of giving or withholding money, position, prestige, affection, punishment, protection, pleasure, and so on)
3. The power of intimidation (as of the threat/act of violence or loss, emotional manipulation, and so on)
4. The power of knowledge (as of skill, information, wisdom)
5. The power of authority (as of self-confidence or the confidence in one's access to another power)
6. The power of focus (as with decision, determination, motivation, and desire)
7. The power of belief (as with assumptions, attitudes, and expectations)

Personal power is the power to direct one's own life and to take responsibility for the effects of doing that. We all use personal power to some degree, and most of us accept responsibility when it works the way that we want it to. However, relatively few people want to take responsibility when it doesn't work out, and relatively many prefer to transfer the authority for running their own lives over to someone else. "Take care of me" seems to be a more popular cry than "Help me take care of myself." "It's not my fault" is a more common refrain than "I'll change myself."

Personal power does not just affect the individual; it may also have social and economic consequences. Take the example of missionaries affecting Hawaiian culture; although the early Boston missionaries have been blamed for many of the social, political, and cultural problems suffered by the Hawaiian people, at least one policy of theirs contributed to many successes by Hawaiians in those same areas.

When the missionaries first arrived in Hawaii in 1820, they immediately sought to turn Hawaiian into a written language. The chiefs of the time knew the value and power of reading and writing from their interactions with Western explorers and merchants, but they wanted to keep literacy restricted to the aristocracy. The missionaries, however, insisted that everyone would learn to read and write or none would. Of course, the primary motivation of the missionaries was to enable as many Hawaiians as possible to read the Bible, but after the chiefs gave permission, the spread of reading and writing was unstoppable. Hawaii became the most literate nation in the world for a long while, with more than eighty independent newspapers created in the Hawaiian language in Honolulu alone. Perhaps the most valuable, enduring effect of providing the Hawaiian people with the personal power to read and write was the preservation of Hawaiian cultural achievements that would otherwise have been lost forever.

Power is meaningless without a purpose, and no purpose can be achieved without power. The larger the purpose, the greater the power, but it doesn't work the other way. You can't accumulate tremendous power first and then set about applying it to a great purpose. It is the purpose that expands the power. When power is used for the good of the many, the person who wields it is remembered with affection through the ages. The most famous king of Kauai was Manokalanipō. According to Abraham Fornander, a researcher of Hawaiian history, Manokalanipō "was noted for the energy and wisdom with which he encouraged agriculture and industry, executed long and difficult works of irrigation, and thus brought fields of wilderness under cultivation. No foreign wars disturbed his reign, and it is remembered in the legends as the golden age of that island." For Manokalanipō, there was purpose behind his power, and for this he is revered and honored even today.

Using power for the purpose of immediate self-gratification is natural. We do that every time we act to increase our comfort, pleasure, or effectiveness. Shopping is an expression of personal power, as is driving a car, playing a game, or making love, but the degree of influence—and therefore the level of power—exhibited in these actions is relatively small. As we involve others in our expression of personal power by helping them to increase their influence, our own power grows. All great religious, political, military, economic, or social leaders have put this idea into practice, consciously or unconsciously. Most have also encountered two major problems based on a misunderstanding of power.

The first problem is falsely associating power with control. This commonly made error is the main reason so many people are afraid of the whole concept of power. Actually, control is just a technique, and not a very good one, for exerting influence. Control requires the threat or the fact of punishment to be effective, and the response to that is always fear and anger. Therefore, the use of the control technique sets up a natural resistance to it. If you look at the surface of a situation, the control technique may appear to be effective, either in a family or a police state, but the underlying resistance is constantly work-ing to undo it. Even if the situation lasts for many years, the control technique will produce a very poor record of achieving the desired results. I will have a lot more to say about this later.

The second problem is using power *against* something. Exerting influence induces change, but the Universe has a built-in resistance to change that helps to keep it from descend-ing into chaos. In all of existence, we can see a constant inter-play between the forces of change and the resistance to those forces. The land resists the powers of water and wind, wires resist the movement of electricity through them, and people resist political reforms that they don't like. We also see constant attempts to reduce resistance in order to make change easier, such as the path taken by molten lava, the shape of a raindrop that makes it move more easily through the air, the structure of a palm frond that allows more wind to pass between its leaflets without damage, the strength of an elephant that permits it to knock over trees in its way, the streamlining of an airplane that reduces wind resistance, and the altering of a lifestyle to accommodate changes in circumstances. Very rarely do we see power used consistently and purposefully to get rid of some-thing, except among humans. Some people are not satisfied with developing their own religious or political system; they have to make theirs the only one by destroying the others. Some people do not want to compete; they want to eliminate the competition. The use of power to willfully oppose, subdue, or destroy another power generates tremendous stresses that only weaken both forces.

"Power over" and "power against" are inefficient uses of power. A far more efficient use is "power to," which is inher-ently creative. The former two are inherently destructive. Sometimes the difference is as subtle as an attitude, but the effects can differ vastly.

For instance, two very different approaches to healing are to treat illness as an enemy or as a behavior. If an illness like cancer is perceived as an enemy, then treatment can take on a warlike approach, with harsh solutions like surgery, radiation, and chemicals becoming the weapons for winning the battle. In addition, any treatment without the power to suppress or destroy the cancer, or to reveal its secrets, is dismissed as irrelevant at best or a hoax at worst. On the other hand, perceiving cancer as a behavior, or the effect of behaviors, leads to the thought that any treatment that changes the behavior of body, mind, or environment may be helpful, and that could even include treatments that are weapons in the enemy approach. The biggest difference is that the war attitude produces far more resistant stress in the body, mind, and environment than an attitude of peaceful behavioral change. The result of that, naturally, is that in the latter, more power is actually applied to the healing and less is needed for overcoming resistance. This is simply an aspect of the physics of energy. Hawaiian healing, by the way, was always oriented toward relaxing and strengthening body, mind, and spirit, and never toward fighting or eliminating illness.

In nature we see abundant examples of rocks, plants, and animals following the path of least resistance. We find it in humans, also, alongside what seems to be the practice of following the path of most resistance. However, the path of least resistance may be so glaringly obvious that it takes a radical shift in attitude to recognize it. A blade of grass apparently has the power to break through a slab of concrete, yet it clearly doesn't have the strength to accomplish this feat. But perhaps it isn't breaking through the concrete at all. Perhaps, using the principle that energy flows where attention goes, it is focusing all of its attention on reaching the sun, and it is ignoring the concrete completely. Perhaps, in the face of such a love, the concrete simply parts to let it through. And perhaps this same idea applies to our human lives. That is to say, perhaps the path of least resistance is the path of love. If this is so, then there is greater power and higher purpose in keeping our attention on what we want and not on what we don't want less on what we hate and fear, and far more on what we perceive as the highest good.

A Practical Program

Now that you have a broader understanding of personal power, it's time to apply it toward achieving success—whatever that may mean for you. To succeed means to accomplish what you want in the way that you want. As important as it is to have a philosophy for success, it is equally as important to have some guidelines for practicing that philosophy.

Here is a sequence of sayings that I use every morning to remind myself of the philosophy, to clear my mind and clarify my purpose, to stabilize and harmonize my feelings and emotions, and to relax my body and charge it up for the day's activities. I remind myself of the seven Huna principles in a way that prepares me to achieve my goals in my own way. I do it as if I were my own teacher. On a busy day I may do it very briefly, but whenever I have the time, I work with it for a while. You can do this by repeating the phrases mantra-style, by writing about them in a journal, or by whatever method suits you. The important thing is to take a moment before your day begins to ready yourself for the success you are creating.

BE AWARE *that the world is what you think it is. Decide that you have the power to succeed.*

Unless you can convince yourself that you have the power to succeed—that you have the capacity or capability—you've lost before you've begun. At the moment, you may not have the experience, the skill, or the knowledge to win, but those things can be acquired. The power to succeed is not something you can get from outside yourself, however. You have to believe it already exists and that it is waiting to come forth. The only way to start believing is to ignore all the inner voices trying to pull you down and to insist to yourself that the power to succeed is real.

BE FREE *because there are no limits. Give yourself the right to succeed.*

Too many people limit themselves unnecessarily because they feel they don't deserve to be happy or successful due to something they did or didn't do in the past. If this is your problem, forgive yourself and move on, or forever be bound by the chains you've put around yourself. It doesn't matter who else says you don't have the right or even that you do have the right. You won't have it until you give it to yourself.

BE FOCUSED *because energy flows where attention goes. Increase your desire to succeed.*

The secret to increasing your desire to succeed is to focus on the benefits of succeeding and to decide that those benefits are really important to you.

BE HERE *because now is the moment of power. Start right now with a will to succeed.*

You can't do anything yesterday, and you can't do anything tomorrow. You can only do something right now. But "right now" is like a foreign country to people who spend most of their time dwelling on the past or the future. If you aren't used to it, it isn't easy to stay centered in the present moment. The way to practice is to consciously breathe, consciously look at colors and shapes, consciously listen to the sounds around you, and consciously touch what is within your reach. And then consciously act, even in the smallest way, in a direction of your choice. The past and the future can be interesting places to visit, but you wouldn't want to live there even if you could. Your real home is here and now.

> **BE HAPPY** *because love is the source of power. Enjoy and acknowledge the good that is.*

If you aren't happy, get happy. How can you do that when so many awful things are going on? Well, Frank Bettger, author of *How I Raised Myself from Failure to Success in Selling*, used the "fake it till you make it" technique, and it worked for him. But I'll give you a simpler way that works for me and for thousands of others I've trained. A very ancient technique, it's called "count your blessings." You do it by actively seeking out and feeling appreciation for all the good things you can find. This includes all the good experiences you've ever had, no matter how minor they may seem; all the skills you've ever learned, including walking, talking, and dressing; all the beauty and wonder in the world around you; all the good deeds done by others that you see and hear about. I'm not suggesting that you pretend bad things don't exist, because this is a practical teaching, after all. But the more aware you are of goodness, the easier it is to deal with the bad.

> **BE CONFIDENT** *because all power comes from within. Always trust yourself.*

You can't trust people to always do what you want because they have their own priorities and agendas, which may or may not agree with yours. You can't trust the world to always be the way you want it to be because there are so many forces and influences at work that may not be moving in the direction you want things to go. But you can always trust that you have the power to change what you can change, to adapt when you're unable to make changes, and to increase your skills by study and practice. One of the best posters I ever saw was of a sailor at sea in his boat, with a caption that read, "You can't control the wind, but you can always adjust your sail."

BE POSITIVE *because effectiveness is the measure of success. Always expect the best.*

Some people believe in preparing for the worst so they won't get any nasty surprises. There are two problems with that: First, they usually get nasty surprises anyway, and second, they seldom get any good surprises. Other people avoid optimism because they are afraid of being disappointed. Let's take a hard look at that: disappointment is being unhappy with a certain outcome. So these people are not planning for success because their plans might not work and then they might feel bad. They are so afraid of feeling bad that they'd rather not feel good.

There's something about this logic that escapes me. Yes, things might not turn out the way you want and you might decide to feel bad. So? If you still want to win, you try something different and start again. I often say that people don't fail, plans do. People just give up or make new plans.

It has been said—very neatly, I think—that "luck is when preparation meets opportunity." If you don't prepare for succeeding, you won't be able to take advantage of the window of opportunity when it opens. Sure, disaster might strike. So you trust yourself to deal with it as best you can when and if it happens, making whatever preparations seem appropriate if you live in a disaster-prone area or work in a disaster-prone job. But if you want to succeed at whatever it is that you've set your mind on, then it's much more important to be ready for success. Expecting the best also has the double benefit of helping to keep you more relaxed while giving you more energy to put toward success.

To recap this program for success: Every morning, while you are still in bed or some time soon after you get up, give yourself the following instructions (modified in any way you like), and think about each one for at least a few moments before moving on to the next.

- **BE AWARE** that the world is what you think it is. Decide you have the power to succeed.
- **BE FREE** because there are no limits. Give yourself the right to succeed.
- **BE FOCUSED** because energy flows where attention goes. Increase your desire to succeed.
- **BE HERE** because now is the moment of power. Start right now with a will to succeed.
- **BE HAPPY** because love is the source of power. Enjoy and acknowledge the good that is.
- **BE CONFIDENT** because all power comes from within. Always trust yourself.
- **BE POSITIVE** because effectiveness is the measure of success. Always expect the best.

3

Designing Yourself

'Ohi ka manu o ke ao
The fishing bird reaps its harvest daily
(Persistent action produces results)

*A*re you happy with your life? Do you ever wish you could be someone else? Don't worry, you will be.

It is a fact of life that people change. Some people let themselves be changed by other people or by circumstances, and some people decide to change themselves in order to change their circumstances.

One of the most famous men in Hawaiian history was a chief of the Big Island named Lono. He was very clever and skilled in many ways, but one nearly fatal flaw in his personality was his readiness to believe the worst about the people closest to him. In one version of his story, he heard that another chief was flirting with his wife and immediately suspected her of having an affair, almost killing her in a fit of rage. Insane with remorse, the chief wandered in the wilderness, followed by a faithful retainer who helped bring him back to sanity. He later heard rumors that this retainer was plotting against him, and he banned the faithful man from his household. Finally, he realized what he was doing to himself and to his chiefdom, and he made the conscious decision to change his thinking and behavior. He became a loving husband, a friend to his retainer, a wise and compassionate ruler, and founder of the annual Makahiki celebration of peace, thanksgiving, and sports events that survives in Hawaii to this day.

In this chapter I am going to teach you a Huna system for consciously designing your own personality. Of course, this idea is contrary to what many people are taught. One of the early ideas in the field of psychology—one that a lot of people still believe in—is that your personality is set by a certain age. Some say seven years old, some say five, some say it's in your teens; whatever they say, the basic constructs of your personality are supposed to be set by a certain age, and there's nothing you can do to change them.

Well, in Huna that idea is not so. The fact is that you *can* change your personality as completely and as profoundly as you desire *anytime* during your life. Implementing the change may not be easy, but the steps are fairly simple. First let's take a closer look at what defines a personality and what goes into changing it.

What Is a "Personality"?

Personality is the sum of all your ways and patterns of thinking and behaving. Emotional reactions, attitudes, habits, likes and dislikes, fantasies, skills, and talents all make up your personality. Psychologists often talk about a person's personality as being one whole, and they talk about different kinds of personality groups that people fall into. Carl Jung divided personality groups into four types, and astrology divides them into twelve.

The Enneagram, another personality-type model, divides them into nine. And I have read about one philosophy that divides them into thirty-three. All of these are purely arbitrary systems, however. You can make up as many types as you want, divide them up any way you like, and come up with something that sounds fairly logical, but there will always be someone who does not fit the system.

In actual practice, really looking at people the way they are and how they act, you will find that individual people have lots of personalities. Which personality comes out at a given time depends on what they are doing and who they are with. For the most part this personality swapping develops spontaneously. As we move through life, we discover that certain behaviors work in certain instances while other behaviors work in other places or with other people; we develop different ways of reacting to different kinds of people and situations as needed.

For example, you may adopt a childlike personality when you are with your parents or in certain relationships where you have learned that childlike behavior helps you to get what you want. When you are with an employer, you act a particular way, and when you are with colleagues, you may act entirely differently. In fact, you can come up with a different personality for all kinds of situations so automatically and spontaneously—so habitually—that you hardly notice that you've made a real shift sometimes. You may have observed the shift in others, though. Maybe you've noticed that subtle, and sometimes not so subtle, change a friend undergoes when visiting his or her parents; maybe your friend doesn't seem like the same person in this environment. This happens a lot because there's a certain set of patterns, or habits of behavior, that operate with the parents. When such a person is out in the world away from home, they don't need or use the same patterns.

Some people call these variations "subpersonalities" as if they were mere appendages to a larger or more fundamental basic personality. While it's true that in some people there may be certain common characteristics between all their personality variations, that isn't necessarily so in others. And I'm talking about people who are generally considered mentally healthy. I have a good friend who was sweet, kind, gentle, and lots of fun to be with. When she fell in love with a nice man, I was very happy for her, and I expected that they would have a wonderful life together. To everyone's surprise, it didn't turn out that way. When she got married, her personality changed radically. She went into jealous rages, and she became abusive, critical, suspicious, and demanding—all behaviors that she had never exhibited before. For some reason, married life brought out the worst in her.

Personality Patterns

There are those who would like to blame past life experiences when something like this happens, but in this case the problem was much more simple. My friend had a personality pattern for friends, which she used with me and with her fiancé. But a husband and wife relationship had a completely different meaning for her. She had another personality pattern for that relationship, learned in childhood from her own family, and it bore no resemblance to her friendship pattern. The problem may have been simple, but unfortunately the solution was not. That's because there were not one but two problems, the first of which was simply that a different set of expectations produced a different personality pattern when she made the shift from engaged to married. The second problem was that she refused to give up those expectations and was therefore unable to change the pattern. Please don't get me wrong; it was not that she was physically, emotionally, or mentally incapable of changing the pattern. It was that she refused to stop practicing the pattern, and that's why she was unable to do so.

As the third principle of Huna tells us, "Energy flows where attention goes." The reverse is also valid. "Attention goes where energy flows." In our present discussion, this means that every time you act in a particular way, you reinforce your reason for acting that way. It would be an inescapable loop except for the fact that you always have the power of conscious choice to move your attention elsewhere, thus weakening the connection between thoughts and behavior.

My friend's real problem was that she *would* not look for an alternative, not that she *could* not. There were plenty of other good marriage relationships that she could have used for models of how to do it differently. For whatever reason of her own, she did not want to do it any other way. And so she stays in an unhappy marriage of her own making.

You Can Choose to Change

Here's a modern proverb for you: *If you want to change your life, you have to change your life.*

Changing your life means changing your self because the self is made, consciously or unconsciously, by you. Your self is what you are today; it is the combination of your thoughts, feelings, and actions. It is not where you were born, nor who your parents were, nor the color of your skin, nor the language that you speak, nor the education or training that you may or may not have had, although these and other things may have an influence. It is, rather, all that you are inside and all that you present to the world. And you can change every part of it.

Personality is a learned pattern composed of relatively small amounts of your potential for thinking, feeling, and acting. You can either keep what you've learned, modify what you've learned, or create something completely new.

There is a lot of familiar precedent for doing this consciously. Good actors will sometimes consciously design a personality for a character so well and so clearly that they step into it like putting on a different set of clothing. Some of them step into a role and never step out. John Wayne was one of those actors. You can tell the difference between how he presented himself in some of his early movies and what he became later. In his case, he gradually created a kind of John Wayne stereotype for himself, probably based on his *Stagecoach* character, and he lived it, on screen and off. He did it so well that practically anyone could mimic him, even badly, and audiences instantly recognized the John Wayne persona.

Angelina Jolie is a good example of an actress who has developed several personas that she can step into as needed. There is the dedicated cop type in *The Bone Collector* and *Taking Lives*; the wild woman in *Girl Interrupted* and *Gone In 60 Seconds*; the cool adventuress in *Tomb Raider* and *Mr. & Mrs. Smith*; the seductress type in *Alexander*, *Beowulf*, and *Original Sin*; and unique ones for special occasions, like her role in *A Mighty Heart*.

Adopting various personas is part of an actor's job, of course, but everyone creates different personalities for different circumstances by happenstance, without any conscious awareness or intent. Their personas come about as a pattern of reactions to events, and to other people's opinions and ideas and actions, rather than from having any clear sense of themselves and what they want to accomplish.

Personalities are usually created unconsciously, but whatever can be done unconsciously can be done consciously, and usually better with more knowledge and technique. Your current personality was most likely created unconsciously, and if it's time for a change, you can create it consciously this time.

Inner Change Produces Outer Change

Anytime you make a change in your beliefs that includes a change in the way you respond to the world or think about yourself, you are producing a change in your personality that will alter your experience. Your life will have changed because you have changed yourself. People will also change how they behave toward you, and even your environment will seem altered. Let me guide you through an exercise that will demonstrate just how simple and profound this can be.

Wherever you are while you are reading this, look around at your environment. Then follow each of these steps, giving yourself at least one minute for each step.

1. Imagine that you are an interior designer (if you are inside) or a landscape artist (if you are outside). How might you redesign the space you are in?
2. Imagine that you are a carpenter. What do you think of the way your space was put together, and what would you do differently (if you are inside)? Or what would you build here if you had to build something (if you are outside)?
3. Imagine that you are a real estate agent (whether inside or outside). What features would you point out to your client?
4. Imagine that you are a fine-art painter. How would you depict the space you are in?

Going through the exercise, you will notice several very important things. First, as you move from step to step, certain aspects of the space will attract your attention and others will not, and this will change with each step. Second, each framework carries with it a special vocabulary, a certain body of related knowledge, and a specialized set of assumptions and expectations that allow various actions to be considered that would not be found in other frameworks. Third, the longer you stay within a particular framework, the more knowledge and ideas will pour into your mind related to that framework. As you identify with different sets of assumptions and information, your personality is modified accordingly.

Is It Time for a New Persona?

Let's define some terms before we go further. Although the words *personality* and *persona* can be interchangeable, for the sake of this discussion, I will use *personality* to mean an unconscious creation and *persona* to mean a conscious creation.

To continue, personalities and personas are very much like the professional frameworks we used earlier because they each consist of patterns of thinking, feeling, and behaving. The only difference is that personalities and personas can be applied within a professional framework, in the same way that an actor can imbue a specific role with a specific persona. Thus, John Wayne could play a tough-but-soft-hearted cowboy or cop, and Angelina Jolie could play an emotional wild woman or a cool adventuress. The persona defines the nature of the role, and not the other way around.

If you are getting the results you want in every area of life, then whatever you are doing is working well. In that case, the only thing you might want to consider is becoming more aware of what you are doing. The more aware you are of the patterns that are working for you, the more easily you will be able to fine-tune them if you wish. Or, if they don't even need fine-tuning, at least you will be able to share them with others more easily.

If you are not getting the results you want, then one part of your plan for self-improvement ought to be the designing of one or more personas.

A question that is bound to come up when you consider creating a persona is whether this isn't just being phony. After all, actors are just pretending to be someone else, and pretending to be something you are not in real life is dishonest. It's a fair question, but it's based on a mistaken assumption. I'm not talking about creating a phony persona. John Wayne created a film persona, and he liked it so much that he made it his life persona. And although John Wayne wasn't even his birth name and his persona was invented, he became it by intentional practice. Even so, John Wayne was not a phony person.

Here is something that may come as a shock: There is nothing sacred about the mass of thoughts, feelings, and behaviors that you have scraped together throughout your life and identify with today. *You* are sacred, as an individual human being, but your collection of thoughts, feelings, and behaviors are not. They are just things that you've haphazardly learned how to do (except for whichever ones you purposely practiced to develop, of course). Whatever cannot be changed is sacred, not because it shouldn't be changed, but because it can't be changed. The fact of your existence cannot be changed. Your experience can be.

The *Haipule* Technique

The first thing you need is a specific technique. In Huna a general technique for creating change is *Haipule*, a Hawaiian word meaning "prayer, blessing, or spell." That dictionary definition is not quite accurate, however. In reality, it's a process for organizing and strengthening one's thoughts, feelings, and behaviors based on the simple theory that by changing yourself you can change your experience. While *Haipule* can be applied to anything, we will use it here for designing your own persona.

The secret of *Haipule* is in its four basic roots: *ha-i-pu-le*. Translated for the purpose of this technique, they mean "energize," "verbalize," "mentalize," and "actualize." Let's explore these action words and the steps involved in each one.

Energize

Increasing your available energy helps to stimulate your organs, strengthen your muscles, nourish your cells, calm your emotions, excite your feelings, and clear your mind. The most usual ways of doing this are by breathing, drinking water, eating food, and exercising. The quickest results come from breathing more deeply, and you can amplify that even further with the use of attention. Try this for one minute:

1. Find something—anything—in your environment that seems to have a lot of energy. Good options are looking at or listening to ocean waves, watching the effects of the wind or feeling it on your body, listening to energetic music, watching active sports, bouncing on a trampoline, or sensing any kind of strong vibration. If nothing else is available, you can look at a picture or video of something energetic.
2. While your attention is on the energy source, inhale deeply for five to ten seconds and imagine that you are inhaling the energy from that source.
3. Then exhale for five to ten seconds, and imagine that this energy is going to a special place in your body where it will be available for use in the rest of the exercise. This could be your brain, heart, navel, spine, or wherever else you like.

Verbalize

Words are useful in helping to direct or redirect our attention. By themselves they have very little power, in spite of all the magical nonsense that is written to the contrary. Directing or redirecting attention can have powerful effects, however, because of that third principle of Huna: "Energy flows where attention goes." And words can play a useful role in this. They evoke associations, associations stir up memories, and memories influence behavior. Try any of the following exercises for one minute:

1. Speak words of praise or admiration related to the persona that you want to create. This could generate phrases like "I love it," "It's good," "That's wonderful," or whatever words seem right to you.
2. Speak words affirming that you have, will have, deserve, or want the persona you want.
3. Speak words directing what you want to happen. For example, "Bring me that," "Create that for me," "Do this or that." Don't bother with who or what you are giving the directions to. It's really yourself.

Mentalize

Some people think that visualizing is the only way to use your imagination. The truth is that imagination can be applied to any of your senses. You can imagine seeing, hearing, smelling, tasting, and touching, and sensations such as pressure, heat, cold, roughness, smoothness, and tingling. Anything that you can experience you can also imagine. And if you can do it vividly enough, which means with enough concentrated attention, your subconscious will accept what you imagine as being just as valid as any external experience. By itself this will not guarantee that you will get what you imagine, but combined with the rest of *Haipule* it will increase the probabilities greatly. Try these variations for one minute each:

1. **Planning.** Using all of your senses, imagine the way you want to be, or how you want things to be, in great detail, as if you are laying out a plan of action.

2. **Remembering.** Using all of your senses, remember in as much detail as possible anything you have done previously that resembles what you now want, or anything that someone else has done that resembles what you now want.
3. **Fantasizing.** Using all of your senses, create a symbolic fantasy of the persona you want, in as much detail as possible. Give yourself the freedom to make it as wild, wonderful, extravagant, and unreal as you can. Sensory detail is more important than realism in this step.

Actualize

This is where you do something physical that is either directly related to the persona you want, or symbolically related. For instance, if you want to develop a more socially oriented personality, you might buy or put on a piece of clothing that fits your new image. Or, if you want to have a joyous, exuberant persona, you might make a picture scrapbook of people at parties and write your name on the happiest ones. Keep in mind, though, that at some point symbolism will have to be replaced with real action.

Now that you know the technique, the next question is, how do you apply it to designing your own persona? You need a system.

Since all systems are arbitrary, according to the second principle of Huna, let me give you an arbitrary system based on Hawaiian concepts as a guideline that you can modify or add to as you please. In this system you can focus on designing three selves: your physical self, your emotional self, and your mental self. For the sake of this exercise, we will discuss each of these aspects separately.

Designing Your Physical Self

"Physical self" refers to your state of health, your energy, how well your body functions, and your appearance. You really can design, or redesign, your physical self using *Haipule*.

A long time ago I attended a workshop, the kind where you get up and share things about yourself with everybody. Into its second day, the workshop was building a lot of positive emotional energy, due to simple breathing and relaxation exercises combined with a complete lack of criticism. At one point the facilitator asked a young woman to get up on stage. She had long blonde hair and a plain face, and she was probably eighteen or nineteen years old. While on stage and sharing, she said that she felt plain and, even more than that, ugly. She wasn't ugly, but she was plain, no doubt about it. The facilitator's approach was to use what the people shared on stage as a means to help free up limited thinking. So, because this young woman said she thought she was ugly, he asked her to say, "I am beautiful." Naturally, this was very difficult for her to do at first, and her face got quite flushed. Even though she had a hard time with it, he kept her up there and had her say this over and over again. His intention, as he explained later, was only to help her become more comfortable with the idea—no more than that. However, in the course of making her statement over and over, there was suddenly a gasp from the audience. Without her awareness, the young woman straightened up, her face began to glow, and, incredibly, she became beautiful.

A very real transformation took place in that woman. It looked like some kind of wave had passed over her face; she actually became beautiful. Afterward, a lot of people wondered out loud why they hadn't seen that beauty before. The answer is that it was because of what she was projecting before. The way she thought about herself was influencing everyone around her. She was not only acting plain, but everyone else was seeing her as she saw herself. Saying those few simple words—"I am beautiful"—affected her subconscious, and that affected the subconscious perceptions of others. You can think of this as a telepathic influence or an emotional response—it really doesn't matter. What *does* matter is that the way others perceive you has less to do with your actual physical appearance than it does with how you think and feel about yourself. And if you honestly believe that you are beautiful, no matter how that belief came about, you will be perceived as beautiful. That young woman, by the way, became immensely popular for the rest of the workshop and beyond.

In terms of *Haipule*, this persona transformation incorporated the four aspects:

- **Energize:** There was a strong field of positive emotional energy and a desire to change on the part of the young woman, or she would not have been at the workshop.
- **Verbalize:** Her affirmation was so unbelievable to her at first that she stopped consciously resisting it after enough repetitions.
- **Mentalize:** There were probably memories of beautiful women being stimulated as she spoke.
- **Actualize:** She was standing on a stage, proclaiming to a group of observers that she was indeed beautiful, and their response reinforced her new self-perception.

All the elements of *Haipule* were there in this woman's experience except conscious intent. But remember: Whatever can be done unconsciously can be done consciously.

Designing Your Emotional Self

One great fallacy people have is that you are what you feel, and it's very difficult to change an emotional pattern as long as you identify with that pattern. Part of the problem, of course, is social and sometimes therapeutic typecasting: "He is an angry person." "She is an anxious type." "He is a manic-depressive." When you begin to label yourself in these ways, you compound the difficulty.

In actuality, these are just behavior patterns, almost always unconsciously developed to cope with some seemingly insoluble problem in life. With conscious intention and an organized process like *Haipule*, any emotional behavior pattern can be modified or replaced. Mind you, I don't promise that it will necessarily be easy or that it won't take long, but it *can* be done, and often more easily and faster than you would believe.

To begin with, you have to decide what kind of pattern you want to create instead of the one you have. For various reasons, in my teenage years I unconsciously developed a serious lack of self-confidence, which worsened with the death of my father. Because of my natural acting ability, I could put on a good front, but inside I was quivering jelly, going way out of my way to avoid any real challenge to my self-esteem. As a result, I majored in pool during my last year in high school and ended up in sixty-fourth place out of a class of sixty-five. (I tried hard to be last, but I wasn't even good enough to be that bad.) I did manage to get into college, and in spite of my desire for higher education, I majored in extracurricular ping-pong and failed my first year spectacularly. My life had bottomed out, and big change was necessary. In my book *Instant Healing*, I give a lot of details about what happened next, so I won't repeat them here. Suffice it to say that I knew I couldn't make the changes I needed to make by myself, so I joined the U.S. Marine Corps with the conscious intention of using it to help create a whole new persona. In a way, my time in the military service became a three-year *Haipule*. If I knew then what I am now teaching in this book, it would not have taken nearly so long (and I probably would not have joined the Corps).

The energy was provided by my desire to change and by the Corps' program of enforced physical fitness. The verbalization involved a daily regime of almost constant mental self-praise, affirmations, and self-directions that helped me get through everything I had to do. The mentalization consisted of lots of careful planning of how to act in different circumstances and confrontations, a great deal of memory-modeling of various movie and fiction characters who had the qualities I wanted to have, and lots of fantasizing about going home as a winner. The actualization was also carried out every day in the form of developing physical and interpersonal skills and increased responsibility. In short, it worked. And when I finally got out and went home, I had the same name, but I was a different person.

You can use what I did to guide your own process for developing your physical persona. Energize with exercise, praise your progress, imagine your encounters, and act the way you want to feel.

Designing Your Mental Self

Although people are changing their minds, trying to improve their minds, and working to expand their minds all the time, a popular belief persists that the mind is more of a fixed entity than the emotions or the body, and thinking differently from your usual pattern is just not right. Because of this, many people are only willing to learn something new or think in a different way if it does not disturb what they are familiar with. And this is because they identify with the way they think. Instead of "I think, therefore I am," which was René Descartes' justification for existence (and which is probably as good as any other), the people I'm talking about would say, "I am what I think." To hear them speak, the beliefs they have about themselves are as sacred as a religious holy place. Many times, when trying to help someone change, I will hear the phrase, "Oh, I can't think like that. That's not me."

Your mind is potentially the most flexible part of you, much more so than even your body, emotions, or spirit The reason is that the primary quality of your mind is your imagination. Developing your mental self means developing the power to focus your imagination in order to expand your awareness, increase your ability to learn more and faster, appreciate different points of view, notice the reactions of others more quickly so you can adapt to them more effectively, and include more patterns of behavior in your repertoire for coping with the unexpected, to name a few.

Once I took a speed-reading course that stretched my mind in ways I didn't expect—ways that have stayed with me because I wanted them to. I have always prided myself on having a flexible mind and a great imagination, but this course kicked me into a broader pattern than the one I had. My father had taught me several techniques for speed-reading, and I practiced those until I could read well above average. The average reading speed of a college student reading fiction or nontechnical materials is 250 to 300 words per minute, and a good reading speed is considered to be 500 to 700. Thanks to my father's training, 800 words a minute became my normal mode.

I didn't take the speed-reading course because I thought I needed it; I took it because of its outrageous claim of being able to teach you to read 20,000 words a minute! Like most people, I could have laughed at the claim and confidently asserted that *no one* could read that fast. Instead, some other like-minded folks and I paid the outrageous course fee and decided to try something new, just to see what would happen.

The course emphasized relaxation, and they taught a simple form of alpha meditation that was effective. But the most important aspect for the speed-reading was the use of your mind to imagine reading faster than most people would think was humanly possible. This was reinforced by "reading" books upside down and backward without being concerned about comprehension. We flipped through pages as fast as possible while imagining that we were absorbing everything. The day of reckoning came with our final test: reading a classic novel at super-speed, followed by a written test for comprehension. My reading speed was clocked at 12,000 words per minute, and a twelve-year-old girl and I tied for nearly 100 percent on the comprehension test. The most curious part for me was that during the test I found myself remembering things I didn't remember reading. Another important part of the course was learning to trust myself.

No one in the course ever made 20,000 words a minute with comprehension, and few ever got as high as 5,000, even after months of practice. Now, 2,000 to 3,000 words per minute with full comprehension is common for me when I put my mind to it. The big lesson here is that the farther you stretch your mind in a short, intensive session, the more stretched out it stays after the pressure is off. Reach your mind to the limits in order to change your mental self, a critical part in designing your persona. This speed-reading experience contained all the elements of *Haipule*—energy, words, imagination, and action. We'll keep using them in the chapters to come.

Designing the Harmony

Designing your physical, emotional, and mental selves is not going to do you a lot of good unless you can integrate them harmoniously. Both ancient and modern Hawaiians with any sense of awareness admire, respect, and seek this harmony, which some call "balance." Usually it is expressed as the need for bringing mind, body, and spirit together. For some, the state of harmony itself is the experience of spirit, and for others, spirit is one aspect, or self, that must be brought in to create the harmony. This is not the place for me to tell you what I think "spirit" means, so I will let some Hawaiians say what they think about it, and maybe you will get some useful ideas.

The authors of *The Art of Lua*, a book on the rebirth of an ancient Hawaiian martial art, have this to say: "In studying, a *haumana* (student) incorporates lessons so that the mind, heart, and spirit are one in harmony and function in unison."

In speaking about her *lomilomi* massage work, Margaret Kalehuamakanoelulu‘uonāpali Machado said, "If your hands are gentle and loving, your patient will feel the sincerity of your heart. His soul will reach out to yours. She'll know you love her and she'll just let go of herself."

And my friend and *hula* master George Naope says about the *hula*, "To me, it is the foundation of life. It teaches us how to live, how to respect, how to share. The *hula*, to me, is the ability to create one's inner feelings."

Now you know how to shake up your personality Hawaiian-style: You use energy, words, imagination, and action to design your selves, and the spirit of *aloha*, of love, to integrate them.

4

The Duplication Effect

No'ono'o ke ali'i, ehu ka ukali
Thought is the chief, activity the follower

In this chapter we are going to talk about a special application of *mana*—personal power in Hawaiian. An understanding of *mana* will help you hone your relationship to energy: become aware of it and learn how to release it, increase it and direct it to your benefit.

Let me start off by saying that the word is greatly misunderstood. *Mana* means "power," although it is often translated in books today as "energy." You may read about *chi, ki, prana,* and *mana* as if they are all the same thing, but *mana* does not belong in that list because it is not energy, not even life energy. *Mana* means power. According to Webster's Dictionary, "power" means "the ability to do or act," and also "authority or influence." Authority, at its roots, means "to create," and it's related to the word *author*, as a matter of fact. So we are talking about creative power, and we are also talking about influence—the power to get something else or someone else to do or act.

Mana has been misunderstood by a lot of anthropologists as well. They have applied the word to what they consider similar concepts in many cultures. Just like *shaman*, a Siberian word that is applied to many places in the world, *mana* is a Hawaiian word that's applied wherever the concept of spiritual power is mentioned. Too often, however, anthropologists try to translate it either as "prestige," for instance, or as some sort of magical energy that primitive people believe in. *Mana* is not prestige; it is the influence that comes *from* prestige. And it is not some kind of magical energy; it is the power to use or influence *any* kind of energy.

Change and Influence Involve Energy

What we are interested in here is the power to change things, or the power to influence things. This is the personal power we are talking about: the power to change or influence your life; the power to change or influence your body; the power to change or influence your relationships, financial condition, environment—whatever it is you are interested in changing.

Naturally, energy is involved in using this power, but it is *directed* energy, not just pure energy. I am going to teach you how to direct this energy in many ways in order to accomplish your desires, but first we need to be more aware of energy itself.

In physics, energy is defined as the capacity to do work, and although the words *energy* and *power* are often used interchangeably, the capacity to do work is not the same as the ability to do and act. You might think that it is a very fine distinction, but I think it is a very important one. In metaphysics, energy is usually defined as "vibration," and the original Greek root of the word means "activity." What we end up with, in a practical sense, is that energy is movement. And we can add to that, in a practical sense, the idea that everything has energy and everything has power. Everything has the capacity to do work, and everything has the ability to influence something else. Everything is moving, and everything can move something else.

Even inside your body, a lot more movement is going on than you may realize. For one thing, your body is a bundle of energy. You have electrical energy flashing throughout your body all the time through your nerves and synapses. Many people think of the blood as slowly moving along, but your blood is moving at incredible speeds all through your body all of the time. That's why drinking a glass of wine or a glass of water can have such an immediate effect. Your cells are vibrating all the time, too. There is tremendous activity within your body every single moment. When you become aware of that energy, one of the things you learn is that you never run out of energy. There is no such thing as a shortage of energy because energy in the Universe is infinite. In one atom of your little fingernail, you have enough energy to keep you going as far and as fast as you want to for many, many lifetimes.

So what happens when you feel fatigued or out of energy? You're not really out of energy. When you feel drained, either because you think that someone else has drained you or you feel drained by your work, you're not really drained. You're under stress, that's all. You've tightened up and blocked your own flow, and you're feeling the effects of that. But if you don't recognize that this is a self-generated energy effect, then you're trying to put the blame on somebody—or something—else. And that is what actually diminishes your power.

You have abundant, unlimited, infinite energy, available all the time, every moment of your life. And if the energy in you is virtually infinite, then think about what's around you. As just one example, water—ordinary water—is in constant movement, even when it seems to be still. The hydrogen and oxygen bonds of water molecules are incessantly reforming themselves, and also forming and reforming patterns or clusters among themselves. When you drink a glass of water, you are literally energizing yourself with all that movement.

As we know from modern physics and ancient knowledge, every kind of energy can be turned into another kind of energy. If you were sitting with a group of people, and you all sang a nice, rousing song that made you really feel good, some of your emotional energy would be transformed into heat. The room, warm as it might be, would get warmer because every kind of energy can be transformed into other kinds of energy. There might be a measurable increase in negative ions and there might be some statical/electrical activity as well. All kinds of things can happen as one kind of energy is transformed into another.

We have this capability as human beings; we're doing it all the time. We take in *poi* and bananas, or meat and potatoes, and we transform them into usable energy, too. You already know how to do that, or at least your body does.

Duplication

Another useful energy/power concept is *lualike*, what I call the "Duplication Effect." Very simply, *lua* means "to duplicate," and *like* (pronounced "lee-kay") means "to be like, to resemble." This is one of the powers of your *Ku*, a Hawaiian term used for the subconscious, or "body mind."

Your *Ku* has the ability to duplicate, but what does it duplicate? It duplicates several things. It duplicates the cells of your body, for instance, and it does a very good job of it. The skin cells produce duplicates of skin cells—they don't grow into liver cells. Kidney cells generally become kidney cells, and so on.

Your *Ku* duplicates and reduplicates the cells and organs of your body all throughout your life; you don't have the same body you had seven months ago. We used to think it was seven years, but it's in about seven months that every cell in your body changes. And some of these changes occur daily, some weekly, some monthly. By the time seven months has occurred, everything in your body has changed. You are physically reincarnating over and over again throughout your life because of this duplication effect.

Your thoughts are included in this duplication as well. Your *Ku* duplicates as nearly as it can whatever you are thinking about. It tries to translate your thoughts into some kind of action or experience, so that, for instance, if you are dwelling on a past memory of something that was unpleasant, your *Ku* duplicates that energetically in the present moment by making you feel bad now. In the same way, if you are dwelling on some future possibility that you're afraid of, your *Ku* duplicates the effects by making you feel that fear, tension, and fright right now.

When your *Ku* cannot duplicate your thoughts and feelings into their direct physical equivalents, it uses "near equivalents." Consequently, body systems often suffer from repeatedly duplicated thoughts and emotions. For example, if you constantly think bitter thought, that's one way to manifest gall bladder or appendix problems. If you constantly struggle with love or self-esteem issues, you may have heart problems. Sexual conflicts may show up as problems in your genito-urinary areas.

The practical aspect of this is that increasing your awareness of energy increases the movement of your energy, because the *Ku* tries to duplicate whatever you are focusing your attention on. And increasing your awareness of the Duplication Effect allows you to redirect your attention in order to *change* the effect.

Relieving Tension

Becoming aware of energy in and around your body is also a good way of becoming aware of tension. If you are not used to how your body feels, then you are probably not sure what tension feels like. Because you've lived with it so long, one of the things you can do is learn how to be aware of your energy and how to move that energy to release whatever tension might be there. I will take you through a simple yet powerful technique for becoming aware of energy and amplifying it. The technique is called *Ho'olapa-i-ka-hā*, which means "to animate the breath" or "to spread life." It's a kind of a breath-energizing technique. Think of it like starting with one- or two-foot swells on Waikiki beach and then increasing them to, let's say, six- to eight-foot swells with the same number of waves. That's amplification. We're going to combine breathing with imagination. Try it for about one minute to start; when you become comfortable with the exercise, it may be beneficial to do it for longer stretches of time.

1. Find something in your environment that is moving—for example, running water, blowing leaves, active children, fish in a tank, a fan. If you can't find anything in your environment that's actually moving, then a photograph or a memory of something moving (like horses or cars) will do. The best effects are with something you can really see or feel, however.

2. With your imagination, feel that same movement inside your body at a location of your choice. This means that if your shoulders are feeling tight and you are looking at running water, you would imagine that running water inside your shoulders.

3. Breathe consciously and slowly, with your attention on the outside movement and the inside movement at the same

time. If this is too difficult at first, let your attention go back and forth between the two. Your attention does not have to be timed to coincide with your breath.

4. Keep this up for one minute at each location in your body that you choose. As an energy-awareness exercise leading up to tension awareness, you can start with your head and then go down your body, spending at least one minute in each area.

Releasing Energy

We just learned how increasing your awareness of energy increases energy's movement. Now we're going to turn our attention to *kala mana*, the power of releasing. When you practice releasing energy, you learn that giving energy increases energy. When we give out energy—through movement, action, blessing, prayer for somebody, getting our mind outside of ourselves or out of where it's locked—then energy increases because of the increased flow. And like any kind of directed energy movement, it can change or influence things.

When I help someone to heal their body, I often start them working on healing someone else, to get that energy flowing out of them. I remember a story about a woman in England who had cancer and was told that she had only six months to live. All her friends gathered together and raised a lot of money so she could go to live in Jamaica. Instead of doing that, she decided, "If I'm not going to live anyway, I'm going to see that this money goes someplace else." And so she put all her money and all her efforts into building hospitals that could help children with cancer. In the process of doing this, she totally forgot about herself, and six months later, she was free and clear of cancer without specifically trying to do anything about it. The transformation came because so much of her energy, which had been locked into herself, was now flowing out of herself. That produced the release by increasing the outward flow of the energy in her body.

In another way, when I've worked with people in helping to improve their financial situation, the focus has been "How can you help others? What kind of service can you provide? How can you better the service that you're doing now, or how can you provide a different service that isn't being done?" In doing this, it moves them out of that place of fear that is inhibiting and blocking energy—out toward a place where more energy begins to flow. And as enthusiasm grows, they find that they have much more energy than they thought they had.

Giving energy increases energy. And when you have an increase of energy, you have more energy to influence with.

Releasing Inhibitions

The word for inhibiting energy is *ka'uka'u. Ka'u* is Hawaiian for fear, meaning "to hold back." Fear is a holding back of energy, and this is what happens when we are inhibiting something; this is the essence of fear.

All fear blocks are energy blocks. It's where energy that would normally move forward—that could be used to change something—is being held back. One way to deal with this is to confront what you fear; another way is to change your mind about it; and yet another way is to simply start moving the energy by taking some kind of action, even mental. Mental movement, focus, and attention will all move energy.

I am going to teach you to practice *ku'upau*, meaning "uninhibited flow." Its meaning also includes bringing an end to complexes and entanglements, releasing, and letting things flow in a different way. A television program I once saw reminded me of this concept. It was about Alexander the Great, starring Richard Burton. According to legend, when Alexander the Great arrived in a certain place in Persia, he was shown something called the Gordian Knot—a huge rope tied in an intricate knot, like one of those cord balls that sailors make, only much bigger. It was said that whoever could undo that knot would become the master of all of Asia, but no one had ever been able to unravel it. Alexander took one look at it, pulled out his sword and sliced it in two; he then went on to conquer Asia. This goes along with a corollary of the second principle of Huna, "There's always another way to do anything." Alexander undid the knot—just not in a way that anyone expected.

In order to teach you how to practice ku'upau, I want to give you an energy-moving technique. It's called *ho'opua'i-waho-ka-mana*, which translates as "cause the *mana* to flow outward." I call it the Radiation Technique. It's a way of moving your mind, a way of directing your mind, or, if you like, simply a way of imagining. You will find this technique very useful in physical terms, as when you have physical blocks such as headaches, a cramped chest, a cramped stomach, a cramped pelvis, or any kind of pain. But it's also good for when you have fear or inhibition of any kind about moving forward, taking action, or doing something different.

1. First, take a nice deep breath, letting your eyes close so that you can be aware of your body and its sensations. Imagine that you have a ball of energy behind your navel. If you want to make it a visual image so that it's a ball of light, that's fine; if you want to simply imagine a feeling of warmth, that's also good; if you want to hear a sound, like a vibration, that's all right, too. Anything will work as long as you can imagine some kind of sensation coming from this focus of energy behind your navel.

2. In the same way that sunlight moves outward from the sun, candlelight moves outward from the flame, or heat moves outward from a stove, imagine that this energy is radiating from your navel. Imagine it radiating from inside your body in all directions: out and front, out and back, off to the sides. Do your best to get that sensation of outward movement. When you have achieved a sensation of outward movement from your navel, you can shift the radiating ball of energy from your navel to the center of your head, inside your chest, in your pelvis, or to any other area of your body that needs release, such as a place of pain or discomfort, or anywhere that's housing strong emotions like fear or anger. Don't put any effort into this. Simply focus on the sensation of radiation. Do it for as long as you like, and then take a deep breath and open your eyes.

3. Pay attention to any changes in your body or your mind, and write down anything significant for future reference.

Some people find that in trying to move that ball of energy around, it was more difficult to move it to some places than other places, and they wonder what that could mean. Often it's an indication of some kind of suppressed awareness in an area associated with a difficult experience. When I say suppressed awareness, I mean a subconscious suppression of memories located in the body. Anyone who has some experience with body work, whether as a giver or a receiver, knows what I am talking about. Sometimes when you release muscle groups, all kinds of memories come out. And with those memories come emotions because emotions follow thought. When memories are such that they stir up emotions that we don't like, the *Ku* suppresses them by tightening the muscles where the memory patterns are stored and thereby blocking conscious awareness of them.

According to one Hawaiian release technique, if you talk nice to the difficult area of your body—pretend that it's alive, aware, responsive, and can listen to you—and then tell it that you appreciate whatever it's doing and that you love it, your awareness of that area will begin to increase. You'll also find that if any memories are released, you'll be better able to change your mind about them in a conscious way.

Sometimes you may get some very dramatic imagery or sensations while talking and listening to your body—like a volcanic effect or a brilliant white light. This has to do with your personal subconscious symbolism, which is a completely different topic to explore. The imagery or sensations may be significant for you, and it may just be the way your *Ku* expresses energy changes.

Although I suggested earlier that you close your eyes while doing the technique, it really doesn't matter once you get used to the process. Some people simply find it easier to do it one way or the other. It's possible to learn how to do it even when you're driving. Most people can talk to somebody, listen to the radio, and think about things already while they are driving. A lot of people even drive from one point to another and never remember the trip! Your *Ku* knows how to do more than one thing at a time, but you have to judge that for yourself.

Helping Others

I have also been asked whether the Radiation Technique would work with another person. In other words, could you use it to help others release their blocks by doing it for them?

The second principle of Huna, "There are no limits," carries the concept that you are connected with everybody and everybody is connected with you since *everything* is connected. We are constantly influencing everybody whether we want to or not, and we are constantly being influenced by everybody whether we want to be or not. However, that influence is always like a matching influence. In other words, if you have a tiny bit of fear about some particular issue and somebody you know has a lot of fear about the same issue, their fear can amplify your fear but only because you have some of the same kind of fear already. It's like a resonance, in fact. If you have no fear about that issue, or if you become aware of such a fear and change your mind about it, no influence happens. So to the question, "Can you do this for somebody else?" I would say, "Yes, to the degree that what you are doing coincides with what they want." Part of the nature of the *Ku* is that it moves toward pleasure and away from pain; that is its natural function. And it's going to be primarily influenced by those things that help it go in a direction where it wants to go. If someone is trying to get a release and you imagine that happening for them, it's like their *Ku* is receiving the helping message from your *Ku*, saying, "Hey, that's not a bad idea. I think I'll use it," and duplicates it. There's that Duplication Effect again.

So it's important to realize that when you think of someone, bless them, pray for them, or send them energy, you're not really doing anything to them or for them directly. Their *Ku* is taking what you are sending, translating it into its own terms, and using it in its own way. Therefore, the more beneficial your message or energy, the more likely it's going to be used. If you would imagine not just the energy radiating but how good that feels, you have an even better chance of having a positive influence. And remember it's always influence; you cannot control anyone.

Control and Influence

Let's take a closer look at control. You can't even control your own body, in the sense of forcing it to do what you want. You may say, "Well, sure I can. I decided to pick up this book and read it." You decide, which means you have a brief imagination of doing it; that's what you do consciously. Your body is what picks up the book, opens it, and translates the symbols on the page into something meaningful. Consciously, you haven't the foggiest notion of *how* to pick up the book or even how to read it. You don't know which muscles to pull, which ones to release, which nerve signals to send, or any of the multitude of things involved in a simple act like picking up a book and reading it. You don't know *any* of that consciously. You can read other books about it till you're a scholarly expert, but you still don't know how to *do* it.

What happens is that you've got to have that little flash of imagination that you call your decision, and then you have to let your body do it. That is not really control in the active sense; that is influence. These words that I am writing are coming out from somewhere and are more or less making sense, but I don't know *where* they come from. I'm a psychologist and I've studied physiology, and I haven't the slightest notion of where these words are coming from. All I have is this intention in my mind, this idea which is like imagination of what I want to say, and my wonderful *Ku* goes and finds all these words, puts them together, and even types them on the page for me. I still don't know how it's done—and no one else does, either.

But I can influence what I write with my thoughts and imagination, and my *Ku* loves me so much that it'll say exactly what I want if I don't get in the way. In the same way, we don't have any control over other people, but we can influence them. This influence is the positive aspect, and the more positive we are about influencing, the more other people are influenced. Yes, it's possible to scare someone, but only if they already have a lot of fear, low self-esteem, and low self-confidence. Fortunately, thanks to the increasing availability of personal development teachings from the field of business metaphysics, more and more people all around the world are learning how to have a high enough self-esteem and self-confidence that no one can influence them in ways that they don't want to be influenced.

Increasing your *mana*—your personal power—is the same as increasing your influence in a positive way. Practice that and share the idea, and eventually we can have a whole world operating in harmony. It's going to take a while, yes, but it has already begun.

5

The Power of Focus

'A'ohe wāwae o ka i'a; o 'oe ka mea wāwae, ki'i mai
A fish has no feet; you who have feet must come
and get what you want
(Thoughts must be reinforced by action)

Mākia mana, or "the power of focus," is an important concept in Huna philosophy because energy flows where attention goes. We are talking about focused attention and the idea that concentration condenses energy. We know this concept from physics: The more you concentrate something, the more you increase its density; the more you focus something, the more power it has in a localized way. However, I don't just mean that on a physical level, with objects and with materials. I'm also referring to a mental level. Concentration condenses energy, and that condensation makes the energy more potent for exerting influence. When we are talking about influencing events in our lives and helping others, concentration is a highly important skill by itself, and its opposite is equally powerful.

Scattered Focus

In Hawaiian, *pūhola* means "dissipation." It's the direct opposite of concentration. An example of dissipated energy happens when people are trying to accomplish a task but can't get their energy together. It goes something like this: "Yes, this is what I'm going to do; here's my goal. Unless, of course, I do that one over there. But I'm really going to do this goal; this is the right one. But I really like that over there, and I hate to give that up; or maybe I'd better focus on this one over here . . ."

A whole life can go on like that, and there's never enough energy given to one goal to bring it into being. Such people may not even recognize what they are doing because they think they are focusing on their goals all the time. And they are; *all* of them all the time. That doesn't work very well for very long. There's not enough condensing happening to make it effective enough to accomplish anything. As the third principle of Huna says, your energy, the energy of like-minded people, the energy of the Universe flows where your attention goes. When you have a focus, things begin to happen. The longer you keep that same focus, the more things begin to happen. Now, this is metaphysical and esoteric, and it actually works! It's saying that your focus on something actually creates a movement in the Universe's energy that brings about the object of your sustained attention. This is going beyond the Duplication Effect of your *Ku*. In a sense, it's the Duplication Effect of the Universe's *Ku*. The subconscious mind of the Universe will also try to duplicate whatever you focus your attention on. So events *can* happen that are amazing and magical, except that we usually toss them into the bin of coincidence. We don't pay too much attention to them, and yet, when these things happen, they're telling us how this world is really working.

Here is an example from my life. In the days before any superstores had reached the islands, my wife and I went to Hilo to look for a chair. Now my wife, Gloria, sweet Scorpio that she is, is very intense when she focuses. When she puts her attention on something, boy, there isn't anything else! This time she wanted a particular kind of a chair—one with a hassock. The first place we looked didn't have it, but she didn't give up. There were a lot of furniture stores in Hilo at the time, but none of them had the chair we were looking for. My wife's desire for that chair didn't waver; she just put it on hold while we went to the town's shopping center for something that I wanted to see. We headed toward the shopping center's main entrance, but then she stopped, saying, "No, let's go through Sears."

"What do you want to go through Sears for? There's nothing in Sears that we want," I said. "Let's go through the main entrance."

"I just feel like going through Sears," she replied.

All right, a happy marriage is compromise. So we walked to the Sears entrance, opened the door, and almost close enough to stumble upon it was the *exact* chair and hassock that she wanted! Without a pause, she went right up to the sales lady, ordered it, and the chair was on its way to our home on Kauai.

If you pay attention, you will notice things happening all the time when you get something on your mind or when you take a special interest in something. You see it in the newspaper, you see it on bumper stickers, you get it in the mail, somebody calls you about it, it appears on television, opportunities arise that are related to it. The results can vary according to the nature of your focus and according to the degree of fear or inhibition you have about it. If you start focusing on a million dollars without a level of high, clear confidence and with a bit of fear and doubt in there, you might get a sweepstakes entry instead. If you sustain your focus, you will start getting what Huna practitioners call "nearest available equivalents" to experience. You'll get the exact experience you want if you have no doubt whatsoever. But to the degree that there is doubt and/or fear involved, the Universe receives a mixed message and delivers mixed results. That's why concentration and clarification of what you really want is very important.

What Do You Want?

When I train counselors, I teach them that the very first thing to say to a client is "What do you want?" This goes back to an ancient tradition of not assuming that you know what someone wants until they state it clearly. You can even find this approach in the Bible. In the book of Luke, chapter 18, verse 35, a scene is described in which a blind man is brought in front of Jesus. The first thing Jesus says is, "What do you want me to do?" Although it seems obvious (because the man is blind, after all), Jesus does not assume anything. He waits until the man has clearly stated, "I want to see."

In helping others, always *ask* and *define* what it is that they want, and then you can help the person achieve that. When I had a counseling practice, it was common for a person to come in with an obvious physical problem but wanting help with an emotional issue. The same is true for yourself. Don't assume that anyone else knows what you want, and don't even assume that you know what you want, until you have spelled it out to yourself with as much clarity as possible.

A lot of people have grown up to be experts in what they don't want; they've been trained quite well in that. But to figure out and decide what it is that they do want ... well, for some people that's a whole new way of relating to the world. And yet it's vitally important because you are *fighting* your way through the Universe otherwise, trying to move away from what you don't want and never moving toward anything.

Unclear objectives, scattered attention—these diminish energy and ability. There is a way to put it all together. One way I like that is a nice contrast to *paholo* ("to dissipate") is a beautiful Hawaiian word called *makakū*. Like many Hawaiian words, it can be interpreted in several ways. Basically, it's a rare word that means "the creative imagination of an artist." By its roots, *maka* and *kū*, it could also have the meaning of "fixed eyes," or "view that resembles something else." As a technique, it means "to imagine what you want." Again, that power, that tool of imagination, is the primary one that you have as a conscious mind. All your other abilities come from the power of your imagination.

A Haipule for Focus

I'd like to take you through a *Haipule*, or technique, for focusing on what you want. For this exercise you can pick something big or something small. I will cover the problem of not knowing what you want later. For now it doesn't matter because I just want you to experience the process. Think of it as a rehearsal, if you like, and pick anything that you don't have right now, even if it's only a beer or a pair of new shoes.

1. Imagine that the air around you is filled with energy (which it is), and imagine that this energy is coming into your body and vitalizing your brain as you breathe slowly and deeply.
2. You are going to use words in the form of narration. Find words to describe to yourself what you are imagining. For example, "There's a thick, glass mug filled with beer sitting on a wooden table in front of me, and I can see and touch the condensation on the glass," or "I am sitting on a

comfortable chair, and I can feel my left foot sliding into a black leather shoe of the latest style." Use words appropriate to whatever you will be imagining.

3. You can use either one or two forms of imagination: realistic and fantastic. Some people can do either one, and some work best with one or the other. Feel free to have your eyes open or closed, whichever suits you best.

   a. **Realistic:** Think of something real that you would like to have in your life—some kind of condition, situation, or circumstance. Use your full imagination, meaning with all of your senses. Imagine it vividly, as real as you can. The way to do that is to imagine what you want in intricate detail. In addition to your visual imagination, use your auditory imagination— have some sound in it: background music if you don't have anything else; the person speaking or you speaking; or some other kind of sound, like the wind through the trees. Make this situation as realistic as possible in your imagination. Imagine the sense of touch where your image is taking place—it could be the position of your hands, your feet on the floor or the ground, the temperature or the feel of the air around you. Bring all of that into your imagination as vividly and as real as you can. And speak words to yourself to confirm and express gratitude for what you want, such as "This is what I want. Thank you." Make the senses as intense as you can—the feeling, the seeing, the hearing. Now relax for a moment and let that one go.

   b. **Fantastic:** This other form of imagination involves doing something symbolic—something that stands for the object or situation you want. For instance, if you want a loving relationship, you could imagine two horses nuzzling each other with great affection, or angels in heaven playing with each other. Imagine something at a purely symbolical, fantastical level. If there is some breakthrough that you want to make, imagine breaking through a wall. If it's your body you want to change, instead of focusing on and imagining your body, vividly imagine a healthy tree, plant, or animal. If it's more prosperity you want, imagine being given the key to a treasure cave and walking in. It doesn't matter exactly what it is; your *Ku* will understand its meaning. Finish the imagination with the same kind of intensity and the same kind of message as before: "You know what this means. This is what I want. Thank you."

4. When you feel the intensity as high as you can get it, let go of it and come back, taking a deep breath; relaxing your body; moving your head and shoulders; opening your eyes; and making some kind of gesture to signify completion, like snapping your fingers, bringing your hands together, or touching your heart.

In carrying out this exercise for condensing and focusing energy, you are using the creative imagination of an artist painting a picture. It's important that you do not try to *push* this into being. If you do this with the purpose of trying to make it happen, the only way your *Ku* understands how to help you is to tighten up your muscles and physically try to push. If there's nothing to push against, you'll end up pushing against yourself, gaining more stress and tension than benefit, and blocking your energy instead of letting it flow.

Trusting the Universe

For this kind of work to be effective, there has to be a sense of letting go and trusting the Universe. The Universe is my general term for the spirit of life, for God, for anything that you believe is the source of everything that happens. Whatever you call it, or whatever you believe, you are not the one who is going to make it happen. Going back to that same idea of control that we talked about earlier, you can't control the happening. You can control your imagination, although you can't even control that if you're uptight. The best way to control your imagination is to keep your body relaxed. The idea, then, is to create more than a picture, but still an imaginary experience, and let it be. That's why I threw in the statement, "This is what I want. Thank you." You are not the one who's doing it. You're really saying, "This is the picture I'm presenting for you, Universe. Bring this into being." The more consistent it is, the more beneficial it is and the better it works. But it stops working completely if you think the picture is making it happen or that you are making it happen. The picture is doing two things only: most importantly, it is helping to increase your expectation, and it is also helping the Universe to work clearly with the energy pattern that you are giving it. If you have a fuzzy picture, you're going to get fuzzy results. This doesn't mean that your imagined desire has to look as pretty as high-definition television. It means that the more clearly you have defined what you want, the clearer your results will be.

You make what you want as clear as you can at any given time, not just during an exercise. It is a growth process, though. You may modify it, but keep in mind that drastic modifications often mean more time to build up other things. There's nothing wrong with that; if you really want to make the change, then go ahead. But energy works in the mental world as it does in the physical by following the principle of momentum. Momentum simply means that energy moving in a particular direction tends to keep on moving unless an outside force acts on it. Once you start to move energy along, it will keep going in the same direction if nothing gets in its way. Fear and doubt tend to scatter it, and a shift—a quick change in direction—is the same as a quick change on the highway when you suddenly veer the car to the right or left. That doesn't mean it's wrong to change direction, but it tends to slow things down.

The idea of clarification is so important that I'm inspired to share an old story about one of my favorite metaphysical teachers, Reverend Ike Eikenkrotter. One day Reverend Ike heard one of his parishioners praying for a Cadillac:

"Please God, give me a Cadillac."

"What are you doing?" Reverend Ike asked.

"Praying to God for a Cadillac," said his parishioner.

"You don't have to do that," said Ike. "God has already created thousands of Cadillacs; Detroit is full of Cadillacs! All you have to do is convince yourself that you can have one."

That's where the real power needs to be applied. In these kinds of exercises, it's primarily yourself that you're working to convince. The Universe doesn't really respond to your pictures or your wishes. It responds to your expectations.

Disappointment

When you build up expectations, don't you set yourself up for disappointment? Isn't it better, as some teachers say, to have no expectations at all?

Well, first we have to define the word. Disappointment is what you feel when you've decided you don't like what has happened. That's all it is. Now think about what that leads to: not doing something because you are afraid you might decide when something happens that you don't like it. That doesn't make a lot of sense if you think about it. Deciding not to act because you might get disappointed is like deciding not to eat because you might get hungry again. Yes, if you don't eat for a while you will ultimately get hungry. Then you have the option to wail and moan, or you can go get something to eat. It's also like being someone who is working at a particular skill, like wood carving. Here you are, carving wood and making your statue, and as you're going at it, you slip and the carving doesn't work. Do you say, "How can I make a different statue out of this?" Or do you say, "Aw, it didn't turn out the way I wanted!" throw down your knife, break your tools, and stomp around? A temperamental artist might do that, but an effective artist doesn't do that often. If you want to be successful and something doesn't turn out the way you want, you realize then that you have to do something differently.

Expectations

Some people try to relieve the stress of not being able to control the future by claiming to have "open expectations," which is just a variation on trying to have no expectations. If we don't have any expectations, or open expectations, then we drift with the tide of life, wherever the winds and waves take us. While it is possible to live like this in a deeply spiritual way, I've met a lot more pieces of driftwood than spiritual models. Mind you, I don't condemn the driftwood life. I'm just more interested in life's sailors, the people with purpose.

Let's stop, reconsider, clarify, remove some fears and doubts, get the energy flowing again, and do it over. It is possible to live a life without any particular expectations in normal terms, as long as you live in the present moment. But if you live in the moment with great love and trust, that's really a kind of expectation. You expect the world to take care of you, you expect things to work out, you expect that whatever happens has its good side and you can make use of it. That's living with expectations in a positive way. So your expectations don't have to be way out there in the future; they can simply be your mode of living. And some people live a beautiful life by letting the Universe fill in the details. Some people are of such a nature that when there are very particular things that they want, all they have to do is to create a feeling of expectation in the present, like someone who just *knows* he or she is lucky or deserving and doesn't have to do anything about it. It's another way to go, and you can try it if you want. You'll know if it's a good way for you because it will work.

Multiple Goals

Can we have different goals for different facets of our lives, or do we need to work on one thing at a time?

What really matters is what your conscious mind can handle. In this life, your subconscious mind and the Universe can both handle an infinite amount of desires. Right now, for instance, your subconscious is running your heart and nervous system; digesting the food you ate; building up your muscles; tearing down some cells; getting rid of waste; organizing the birth, nourishment, repair, and replacement of billions of cells; and so on without getting out of breath. You're not going to overload your subconscious unless you start thinking in some way that engenders fear or anger. It's your conscious mind that determines how much can you handle consciously. Generally speaking, it works better for your conscious mind if you can divide your goals into groups of threes and fours. Psychologically, most people are supposed to be able to handle as many as seven concepts at a time, and that's a strain. People seem to work much better with three or four things at most, and that includes other people. One way to handle that is to take the areas of your life and divide them into three or four items: "OK, here are my main goals: health, wealth, happiness, and success," and then under each of those, "For health I want to take care of this, this, and this. For wealth I want this, this, and this," and so on. This is the kind of organization that the conscious mind loves, and it is going to help you keep track of these things better. You can have as many as you want, and if you organize them in some way, they'll be easier to remember and manage. This is just a suggestion, but it does work pretty well.

Another effective suggestion involves having one overall purpose or direction that you decide upon and then fitting everything else into that. For instance, if you say, "My overall purpose is to be a healer," you fit in everything else that you want under the one general thing and that helps keep you on track. This way your whole life is guided by your primary concept of yourself or your direction. As an example, you could plan on taking a course that would help you be a better healer, you could focus on a car to help you do more healing for more people, or you could budget for a television because that will help you relax (a relaxed healer is a better healer).

As this chapter has discussed, focused attention is a skill well worth developing and honing. Of all the things I have learned in my life, this concept and practice has been the most consistently useful. Try it and see for yourself.

6

Being Centered in the Present

Noho ka mana i kēia manawa
Power resides in this moment

We've learned that, according to the Fourth Principle of Huna, now is the moment of power. *Manawa* is a word that has to do with time in general. Its roots, *mana* and *wa*, can be translated as "time of power." When I was first learning the Huna knowledge, this word gave me some trouble because I didn't get the connection with the present moment. Then I was reminded that in the natural Hawaiian language there is neither past tense nor future tense. Everything that happens is relative to the present moment, either finished, happening, or unfinished. Therefore, in Hawaiian all time is present time. I was given two more connections as well: A second meaning of *manawa* is "affections, feelings, emotions," which dwell only in the present moment. And a third meaning is "anterior fontanel," the place on top of your head where your skull bones come together. Symbolically, this is also your connection to Spirit, in the now.

In this chapter you'll learn to center yourself in the present moment in order to increase your effectiveness in every area of life.

The Power of the Present

As a time of power the present moment is the only place where we can act effectively and where we can gather, amplify, and focus energy for our purposes. We can't do that in the past or the future without being there "in the present." When we try, we have less available energy and everything becomes harder to do. Try this experiment:

1. Find a fairly heavy object that is possible to lift with effort, like a large crystal or a heavy chair.
2. Think about something you were doing in the past—yesterday or before—as clearly as you can. Then, without looking directly at your heavy object, pick it up and be aware of how heavy it feels. Put it down.
3. Next, think about something you plan to do tomorrow or after, and pick up the object in the same way with the same awareness. Put it down.
4. Finally, put your hands on the object and feel its texture and temperature, and look at details of its color, shape, and position. Pick it up and feel its heaviness. If your focus has been good on all three attempts, you will notice that by the third time the object will feel much lighter, or you will be able to lift it higher with greater ease.

This exercise helps to show that the more we can learn to bring our senses into the present moment, the more easily we can influence the energies around us—physically, mentally, and emotionally.

Increasing Physical Presence

Being in the present offers tremendous benefits. By bringing your awareness fully into the present, you will be able to accomplish more physically with less effort. You will be able to run faster and farther, recover more quickly during periods of rest, and lift more with greater ease. You will see better, hear better, and breathe more effectively. Your range of smell will increase, and even food will taste better. All of your senses will be enhanced with more focus on the present, and everything you do to improve your body will have better results. With present focus, even a simple exercise will do more for you than vigorous exercise with your attention elsewhere. Here is a simple one you can do at almost any time. I call it "The Shaman Bounce."

1. Stand up with your feet in line with your shoulders.
2. Gently bounce up and down on the balls of your feet for about thirty seconds.
3. Stop and pay attention to what you feel. Commonly, people feel tingling or currents of energy in their body, and/or they start breathing more deeply and easily. It also helps to clear your mind if you are doing mental work and need a break.

Increasing Emotional Presence

Emotional calm is another valuable benefit from being more in the present.

Two things disturb us emotionally more than anything else: the past and the future. Nearly all of our fear comes from remembering past pain or danger and projecting it into a future possibility. And nearly all of our anger comes from remembering past wrongs and projecting them into the future, too. I'd say that 90 percent of our present moment experience contains nothing to be fearful or angry about. Yet, even one small incident involving fear or anger can color our whole memory of a much longer period. I know of people who think of a month-long vacation as having been a disaster because one person that they encountered for one hour on one day made them angry. And, of course, they would never go back to that place because someone there might make them angry again, even though the rest of the vacation had been quite satisfactory. One of my friends, who had flown thousands of miles by plane, had a scary experience in a small plane during a storm on a short trip and vowed never to fly again. Instead of remembering all the times he flew safely, he locked his attention onto the one time he felt he almost died, and he projected his fear of that onto every possible future flight.

While you are fully centered in the present moment, however, you are not thinking about the past and you are not worried about the future. In the moment, unless you are currently experiencing some kind of traumatic or upsetting situation, there is nothing to make you feel fearful or angry, and so your body relaxes, your emotions calm down, and your mind clears. There are times when we need to access memories and there are times when we need to think about the future, but there are also times when we just need to be at peace with ourselves and the world around us. This next exercise is a simple technique called i ʻānō, which could be translated as "being here."

1. Look around you and be aware of colors. In this order, pick out all the whites you can see, then the reds, the oranges, the yellows, the greens, the blues, the violets, and the blacks. Next, look at all the straight lines and then at all the curved lines. Finally, look at the shapes of objects and how they relate to each other in space.

2. Listen to all the sounds you can hear, first high ones and then low ones. As you listen, you will probably hear more and more sounds that you didn't notice at first. Then listen to all of them again, and try to be aware of how what seem to be single sounds at first are often made up of several other sounds.
3. Touch things. Feel their shapes, their relative softness and hardness, their texture, their differences in temperature, their flexibility, their weight.
4. Go back and forth between these three senses—seeing, hearing, and touching—for as long as you like. You may also want to include smelling and tasting.

Some people will find this easy and enjoyable, because they are used to being present. Some people will find it easy and boring and won't do it for very long because they have rules that say this kind of activity is neither useful nor interesting. Some people will find it very disturbing, perhaps even scary or painful, because they automatically switch into unpleasant memories that associate sensory awareness with pain. Some people will find it fascinating and exciting because they've never thought of doing it before. All people, if they do it long enough and often enough, will discover three things: (1) the release of stress and tension that they may not have known they had; (2) an increased feeling of energy, vitality, and well-being; and (3) an expansion of sensory awareness that will change the way they think about the world.

Increasing Charisma

Charisma is another benefit of being more present. Defined as "that special spiritual power or personal quality that gives an individual influence or authority over large numbers of people," charisma is actually a product of the strength of your emotional energy field. Typically, a naturally charismatic person is one who has unusually intense sensory perception. Often they are very emotionally expressive, but not always; they do not know why other people respond so strongly to their presence; and they don't know what to do about the attention—and may not even like it.

Whatever can be done unconsciously can be done consciously, if we know what we're doing. The way to increase your charisma in a positive way is to increase your sensory awareness to a high degree and to be in a good mood. Here is an experiment you can do to increase your charisma and gauge the effects:

1. Do the sensory practice described above.
2. Feel as good as you can about yourself and everything around you.
3. Go for a walk among people, staying present and feeling good.
4. Pay attention to how other people respond to you.

I'm not going to give any guarantees, but to the degree that you do this well, you will typically experience more people smiling at you and saying hello and people being more helpful than usual.

My wife and I had once started on a long European tour only to discover at the first major airport that our whole itinerary, including reservations and upgrades, had disappeared from our airline's computers. The ticket person serving us was not in a good mood and seemed reluctant to do much for us. My wife and I both brought ourselves immediately into the present moment, vocally expressed appreciation for every tiny little step the woman made in our favor, and silently praised and admired her and each other and all the good we could see around us. Also, in that moment, we decided—without any evidence whatsoever—that everything was working out perfectly. We did not allow a single thought or word of recrimination or worry to enter our minds or mouths. The effect was that, gradually, the woman began going more and more out of her way to help us, as if she were taking on our problem as a personal challenge.

Finally, she had reconstructed our whole itinerary, complete with better upgrades than we had started with, and she seemed genuinely happy that we were happy, too. The most significant thing is that we didn't *do* anything to influence her. We simply became very present in very good spirits, and she responded to that. Good charisma can be extremely helpful in many situations.

Increasing Mental Presence

When you are present mentally, three important things generally happen: (1) you notice more; (2) you make correlations between things that you notice more quickly; and (3) your intuition increases.

It's quite amazing how many people walk through life hardly noticing anything around them. That's usually because they are lost in their own thoughts of past, future, and elsewhere. When you notice your surroundings, life becomes a richer experience. Yes, it's good to stop and smell the roses, but there is so much more to experience and learn about. Noticing what's around you is also useful because it can allow you to avoid danger and problems without having to use fear.

At one period in my life I was stubbing my toes so much that I decided to do a study of it. After all, I reasoned, my body was aware of my environment and knew very well how to avoid chairs and rocks and such without my conscious help. I had already demonstrated this by practicing total body trust and running through rocky fields without looking and without stumbling. And this ability of my body was evident in the very fact that I could drive through heavy traffic while thinking about something else. So why was I stubbing my toes?

Over time, I noticed that the only time I stubbed my toes was when I was thinking of something else in a particular way: it only happened when I was remembering or projecting an experience of walking in a different direction than I was walking in at the present moment. My loving *Ku*, trying to duplicate my thoughts, moved me in the direction of my mental path, ignoring my current physical environment. The frequent result was toe stubbing. Since that discovery, I stub my toes much less often and never get mad at myself for doing it. I just do the "Repetition Technique" of moving my foot back and forth toward the object I stumbled against and take it as a reminder to center myself in the present. (For more on the Repetition Technique, see my books *Urban Shaman* and *Instant Healing*.)

The ability to make correlations between present experience and present knowledge is extremely useful. It is one thing to notice something, and it is something more to interpret what you notice in a way that brings wisdom instead of just knowledge. The first merely involves awareness, while the second involves awareness plus recall plus imagination. The fictional detective Sherlock Holmes is the symbolic model for this skill, but any kind of detective in any field makes use of it. And it is one of the most practical skills that anyone can learn.

I once received an email with a wonderful poem that perfectly fits this topic. The poem is "Autobiography in Five Short Chapters" in the book *There's a Hole in My Sidewalk* by Portia Nelson (reprinted with the permission of Beyond Words Publishing):

•••••• 88 ••••••

Chapter One

I walk down the street.
> *There is a deep hole in the sidewalk.*
> *I fall in.*
> *I am lost ... I am helpless.*
>> *It isn't my fault.*
> *It takes me forever to find a way out.*

Chapter Two

I walk down the same street.
> *There is a deep hole in the sidewalk.*
> *I pretend I don't see it.*
> *I fall in again.*
I can't believe I am in this same place.
>> *But, it isn't my fault.*
It still takes me a long time to get out.

Chapter Three

I walk down the same street.
> *There is a deep hole in the sidewalk.*
> *I see it is there.*
> *I still fall in ... it's a habit ... but,*
>> *my eyes are open.*
> *I know where I am.*
It is my fault.
I get out immediately.

Chapter Four

I walk down the same street.
> *There's a deep hole in the sidewalk.*
> *I walk around it.*

Chapter Five

I walk down another street.

Here you can see clearly the transition from simple awareness to awareness plus recall, to awareness plus recall and imagination, and finally to the combining of all three into wisdom.

Perhaps one of the greatest benefits of mental presence is increased intuition. Whenever you put your full attention on something that you have a great interest in, energy channels are opened up between the object of your attention, your related memories, related objects, and the *Kus* of others who have knowledge of or interest in the same thing you do. Information begins to flow along those channels like radio or television content flows along the specific frequencies of electromagnetic waves. This often happens spontaneously if your focus is clear, but if you also hold in your mind an intention to know something, it happens more than often.

This can also happen, of course, without even being in the present moment. I wrote a novel about Atlantis (unpublished as yet) that was based on a dream I had, and the more I thought about my story, the more details leaped into my mind that had not been in the dream. I know from the writings of other authors that this is a common experience, even for nonfiction writers. But it also happens when you are engaged in solving any kind of physically centered problem. To the extent that you are clearly focused on the problem at hand, there comes a moment when knowledge and logic fail to produce results, and a sudden leap of "knowing without knowing" occurs—or help comes from unexpected quarters. Faced with an emergency need to reorganize a wireless connection between two computers in my home office, I found myself without a sufficiently long phone cord to the base station. On impulse, without thought, I went into a storage area, put my hand into a box that I hadn't looked at for a long time, and came out with an extra long phone cord from a previous office.

Since I had no conscious recollection of the cord being there, my *Ku* must have guided me. Before I organize a messy library, I sit in the room, focus on the present with intent, and a simple plan appears in my head from somewhere beyond *Ku* memory. Planning a workshop tour with an empty weekend, I focus on the present with intent and someone emails me with a proposal. The potential uses for such a phenomenon are endless. Give it a try.

Accessing Extra Energy

Just being more aware of the present moment is energizing, but it's possible to amplify your energy far beyond your normal focused potential and to expand your potential with regular practice, just like learning any other skill. When I first learned how to ski, I was falling all over the beginner's slopes. But with practice came confidence and experience, and soon I was able to hold my own on some of the advanced slopes. My skiing potential had increased far beyond what I had started out with, and the same happens with energy practice.

We can learn how to absorb energy from a source in our environment for the purpose of increasing our *mana*, our influence, in several different ways: from natural sources, from organized sources, and from self-generated sources.

Although I used the term *absorb* in the previous paragraph, it's really more like induction. *Induction* is a term used in science to describe the process by which the electromagnetic field of one object can "induce," or influence, the generation of a similar field in a neighboring object without contact. As often happens, scientific principles of energy can sometimes apply to human energy as well as the energies studied in physics. The easiest way to scientifically demonstrate the induction effect is by holding a fluorescent tube, lit by connections to an electrical source, near another fluorescent tube without any connections. When the unconnected tube lights up, which it will, it seems like magic.

One way to demonstrate this effect with human energy is by using a "muscle meter." This is a simple mechanical device with a dial showing pound of pressure on top and two handles below that you squeeze together. I participated in a 1980s laboratory experiment at the University of California at Davis in which several subjects were measured for handgrip muscle strength in three different scenarios: (1) without holding anything in the other hand, (2) while holding a glass of ordinary water in one hand, and (3) while holding a glass of water that someone had strongly imagined as being filled with energy. The study was double-blind (meaning that neither the experimenters nor the subjects consciously knew which objects were energized and which were not), and the results were consistent. Muscle strength increased significantly in every case when the subjects were holding an energized object in their free hand and not at all when they were holding the neutral object. This happened even though the energized object was held on the third trial for each subject, when muscle strength might reasonably be supposed to have diminished due to muscle fatigue. The field of the energized object induced an amplification of the energy field of the subject, increasing muscle strength as a side effect.

Energy Locations

All over the world, quite different cultures at quite different times in quite different areas have located places where the natural energy was more intense than elsewhere, and the people of these cultures use those places for healing and for magic (which only means they use them for energizing their thoughts about accomplishing something). In Hawaii there is a place called *Pu'u Loa*, usually translated as "Long Hill," but which also means "Strong Desire." A specialized class of experts used that area to carve magical symbols, or petroglyphs, into the lava rock as a means of focusing their desires, or a client's desires, to manifest something. Lots of surrounding areas look the same on the surface, but only that particular area was used for this. In Kraków, Poland, one castle courtyard's wall is marked with a long, dark stain caused by thousands of people through the centuries who have come there to lean against the wall and "absorb" the healing energy that is said to radiate from a large rock below the ground. While I was there I saw a whole busload of people come there to do just that. Many places like that exist in many countries. If you can travel to such a place, you can take advantage of its special energy by being as present as you can and thinking thoughts of what you want. However, if traveling to such a place is not feasible for you, there is no need to despair; a lot of other possibilities exist.

Connecting with Energy

Connecting with energy sources is a great way to harness the power of the present. The best place for doing this is anywhere out in nature. Trees are loving beings that love being hugged and also have a powerful energy field. So do human beings, by the way; if you know a powerful human being, hug him or her, too! Human fields and tree fields are similar in this respect: if you get into a peaceful, present space and lean against one or the other, stand between two of them, or sit within a circle of them, you'll get all the benefits of energy amplification. In both cases you'll have more energy flowing, your thoughts will be more clear and powerful, and you will feel calm and relaxed. Other natural places for this are caves, waterfalls, and the tops of hills and mountain ridges. If you know how to use a dowsing rod you will be able to locate even more.

Organized sources of extra energy refer to natural or man-made objects that are arranged or put together in such a way that an especially strong energy field results. Such a field can be used to amplify your own energy. Here are some readily available sources that you can use for this purpose:

1. A circle of eight quartz crystals, large enough to sit in, with all the points directed inward.
2. A so-called "space blanket" made of mylar and aluminum, generally used for camping to maintain warmth in cool weather. This generates quite a strong result due to an "energy field effect" created by the insulating and conducting layers, making it somewhat like a capacitor (see my book *Earth Energies* for more details). The easiest way to use it is to sit on it, but you could sit under it as well. My preference is for the more durable, nylon-reinforced version.
3. Any "circle" of three or more granite rocks at least six inches in diameter. Granite is an especially good energizer due to its composition of hard minerals such as quartz, feldspar, augite, and hornblende. Granite often has a magnetic field that can be detected with a compass. I first learned this while doing energy tests on granite sarcophagi in the Cairo Museum.
4. A rod made of any material, such as wood, copper, plastic, or glass, cut into lengths that are multiples of five inches (or 12.7 cm). The best results come from holding a rod in each hand, or sitting in the middle of a triangle of rods arranged on the floor or the ground. Three twenty-five-inch rods (63.5 cm) will work well for this (my book *Urban Shaman* offers more details).

Self-Generated Energy

We can definitely be influenced and charged up by the energy sources in our environment—trees, stone circles, crystals, other people, and many other kinds of things but we also have an amazing ability that's been used by shamans from time immemorial: the ability to use our own imagination to create an extra energy source with any object. In many times and places these sources are called amulets and talismans, but we can simply call them good luck pieces. With this in mind, I'd like you to try a Hawaiian technique called *ho'omanamana*, or "empowerment."

1. Pick up some object that you have with you or near you right now. It could be a penny, a pen, a piece of jewelry, anything that you want.
2. Hold it in your right hand. (The right hand is a symbolic area for giving out energy.)
3. Decide that the object you're holding has the power to give you energy and good luck (throw good luck in just for the heck of it). First of all, understand that this is a decision that you make. Don't let yourself be bothered at all by the questions of whether it is true or not. It's true right now if you decide it is, so just play the game for now. Tell yourself, "This object has the power to give me energy and good luck."
4. Now take a deep breath, and with every breath that follows, inhale energy from the Universe and exhale that energy into the object. Use your imagination so that you can feel the warmth, feel the heat, and feel—or perhaps see—the object being charged up with light or heat (or whatever you like). And it's not being filled up temporarily; its very molecular structure is being altered so that it can absorb, maintain, and keep more energy. Decide that

you are changing the energy pattern of the object as you do this. Charge it up, and when you get a feeling, a sensing, or an imagining, decide, "The pattern's set; it's done."

5. Relax your hand, take another deep breath, and transfer the object over to your left hand. Now this object is an object of power because you've made it so. Feel the energy from that object with your left hand. Feel it moving into your hand and moving up into your arm, charging your body and expanding around you. As long as you remember it and as long as you remind yourself, that object will be a source of good luck and energy for you.

"Wait a minute," you say. "That's just because I believe it." Absolutely true. If you do what I've just suggested on a regular basis, reminding yourself every day of the power and purpose of that object, it will serve as a constant stimulus and reminder to your *Ku* to charge itself up whenever you are touching it, holding it, paying attention to it. In that way, you create your own power object, just like that. And you are the source.

Hawaiian Time

People who come to Hawaii to stay for a while soon learn about something that locals call "Hawaiian time." This refers to the common experience in Hawaii that things don't usually happen when you expect or want them to. Hawaiians in particular, but also locals of any background, may show up late for appointments—or not at all—and community events rarely begin when they are "supposed" to. Newcomers have a tendency to blame it on laziness or disrespect, but that isn't the case at all. It's really a question of values.

In Hawaiian culture, still today, the most importance is placed on family obligations. In short, family comes first. For this reason, many Hawaiians and other locals who have absorbed the culture are very reluctant to commit themselves to be at a specific place at a specific time because a family obligation might cause them to break a promise. Hawaiians typically do not like to break promises. When you consider that close friends are usually treated like family members, the number of possible obligations increases quite a bit. As far as community events are concerned, delays are probably most often caused by people taking so much time to exchange greetings and news with family and friends.

What does this have to do with our current topic? It's a reminder that people are more important than clocks; relationships are more valuable than appointments or deadlines. We have the choice of letting time, worries about the future, and regrets about the past run our lives, or we can make sure that quality living defines us. Your life will not be enriched by the number of times you've been on time; it will be defined by the time you've spent enriching others.

Love Your Way to Success

Kō ā uka, kō ā kai
Those of the upland, those of the shore
(Share so that everyone's needs are met)

You have learned that when you put your attention on something with intent, energy flows in the direction of your intention, and that energy attracts others with a similar intention. It could be compared to the fact that whenever electricity flows through a wire, a magnetic field is generated around it. When you add some form of love to your intention, it is like increasing the amperage—the flow—of electricity, while expanding the magnetic field at the same time. Love intensifies energy and is therefore a very powerful influence: the greater the love, the greater the influence.

It's good to have an understanding of what I mean by love, because in Hawaiian it is much clearer than in English and other languages. The Hawaiian word for love is *aloha*. The root *alo* means "to be with." It also means "to be present," which means to be with someone or something in the present moment. *Oha*, the next root, is "joy," particularly the kind of joy you have at greeting someone or something, so *aloha* can be translated as "to be happy with someone or something in the present moment." An additional meaning of *alo* is "to share," as in to share an experience, and *ha* is "life energy, breath, life spirit." This aspect of *aloha* is "the joyful sharing of life," and this is also love.

When we can love in a way that increases the free flow between us and something else, influence intensifies, and because of love's nature, the influence is positive. If it weren't, there would be fear, anger, doubt, or control, and it would not be love energy anymore. It would be fear, doubt, anger, or control energy, and each of those generate resistance to the flow. To use the electrical analogy again, love turns your wire of focused purpose into a superconductor.

One of the things that increases energy tremendously and influences change in your life, or in the world around you, is what we can call in Hawaiian *mamake*, or desire. But desire is a tricky concept. In Hawaiian there are lots of different words for various kinds of desire. What we're talking about now would be more akin to motivation. It's not a grabbing kind of desire, or a "got to have that" / needing kind of desire. Instead it's a loving kind of desire, like "Hey, I want some ice cream because I love ice cream!" It's always easier to get something when you have that kind of love for it.

Whatever you love will increase and be drawn into your life (as will whatever you fear). But whatever you love in the sense of using a positive, flowing intensification of energy will flow and manifest more abundantly. People who love their work, or who love doing their particular skills, are usually highly skillful and successful at what they do. When I say successful, however, I mean successful at doing the part that they love. There are some people who are very successful at performing a skill but are not very successful at making money with that skill. That's because they don't have the same kind of loving relationship with money as they do with the skill. Those are two separate factors, but a lot of people don't realize that. You do not get rewarded for your talent alone. You get rewarded to the degree that you're able to love yourself enough to accept reward, or to the degree that you love reward; it's one of the two. To paraphrase an old American proverb: If you build a better mousetrap the world may beat a path to your door, but those who come won't necessarily buy any mousetraps unless you have a good relationship to money.

It isn't enough to know about love, however. Unless you have a practical way to apply it to your success, it is only a nice idea. One of the most practical ways to make love work for you is by using the power of blessing. You may already be familiar with the idea of blessing, perhaps from my booklet, *The Aloha Spirit*, or from one of my classes or courses, but I am going to expand on the idea in order to help you expand your use of it.

You may have witnessed or experienced the muscle test we use to demonstrate the power of blessing. This extremely interesting phenomenon demonstrates that blessing is not just spiritually good, it's physically good as well. When you bless someone or something—that is, when you give compliments, praise, thanks, or goodness in some way—your subconscious responds by relaxing your body and increasing your energy flow. Even though you've directed the blessing to someone or something else, you benefit physically. It's easy to demonstrate this with muscle testing in the following way:

1. Have a partner stand up and raise his or her arm straight out from the shoulder to the side.
2. Tell your partner to hold the arm up strong when you say "Hold," and then push down smoothly on the person's wrist

so you can get a sense of her normal strength. Don't push down all the way—you are not trying to overcome her strength; just push down enough so you can gauge the resistance.

3. With your partner's arm up, have her silently criticize someone and then let you know when she has done it by nodding her head. When you see the nod, say "Hold" and push the arm down again. You will find that the arm comes down easier this time, often dramatically so. This is because the person's subconscious has taken the criticism personally. (Remember the second principle of Huna: "There are no limits.")

4. Do the same test again with the person giving a compliment to someone this time, and you will find that the arm has grown stronger, often much so, because the subconscious has taken the compliment personally, has relaxed, and has freed up more energy to resist with.

Basically, criticisms of yourself or others cause your body to tense, and compliments to yourself or others cause your body to relax. Curses cause stress, blessings reduce it. Using blessings alone can improve your health tremendously, and sometimes that's all that's needed. What do you do when someone else criticizes you? The most efficient and effective thing to do is to immediately, aloud or silently, give yourself a compliment. You can bless your way to success in many ways.

So many people have problems with their relationships, and yet a very easy and workable solution is available. No matter what kind of relationship it is, nor what the intent when you communicate, the fact is that if you give more criticisms than compliments, you tend to destroy the relationship; and if you give more compliments than criticisms, you tend to enhance it. Nagging is deadly to a relationship because it is simply overt or implied criticism, and it doesn't work to make the person better or you happier. If there is any person or group of people that you don't get along with, it is because you have a critical attitude toward them. You get along with whomever you do because you ignore faults (or at least don't consider them as important as the person's good qualities) and you compliment the good qualities. In other words, you bless more than you curse, by words or behavior. Here's a thought that's simple but true: If you want to be totally in love with someone, see and acknowledge only that person's good. To the degree that you don't, the relationship will suffer. So you can bless your way to success in love, too.

Success in your career works in the same way. If you truly love all aspects of it and if you only bless it, then you will be successful in it. Some people experience what is called "burnout" in their jobs. Their ambition disappears, their desire to do a good job disappears, and their job can even make them sick. The problem is as simple as the solution. For whatever reasons, justified or not, such people have begun to curse their work to the point where they give it practically no blessings. The subconscious naturally resists being there but the conscious mind insists, usually for economic reasons, and the result is burnout. The solution? Either find a job you can bless or start blessing the job you have. Even when you haven't reached the burnout extreme, you can use blessing of your work to improve your efficiency and increase your enjoyment. And when you love your work and you do it well, the rewards will increase, too. Just remember that you don't have to bless everything about your work—just the good parts. And make sure that you find more good parts to bless than bad parts to curse.

To help you in your use of this technique, I'd like to share an excerpt from my booklet, *The Aloha Spirit*, for your ready reference. Remembering that a blessing consists of admiration of goodness, affirmation of goodness, appreciation of goodness, or anticipation of goodness, here are some ideas for blessing various needs and desires. Apply them as often as you like, wherever you wish.

- **Health:** Bless healthy people, animals, and even plants; everything that is well made or well constructed; and everything that expresses abundant energy.
- **Happiness:** Bless all that is good, or the good that is in all people and all things; all the signs of happiness that you see, hear, or feel in people or animals; and all potentials for happiness that you notice around you.
- **Prosperity:** Bless all the signs of prosperity in your environment, including everything that money helped to make or do; all the money that you have in any form; and all the money that circulates in the world.
- **Success:** Bless all signs of achievement and completion (such as buildings, bridges, and sports events); all safe arrivals at destinations (of ships, planes, trains, cars, and people); all signs of forward movement or persistence; and all signs of enjoyment or fun.
- **Confidence:** Bless all signs of confidence in people and animals; all signs of strength in people, animals, and objects (including steel and concrete); all signs of stability (like mountains and tall trees); and all signs of purposeful power (including big machines and power lines).
- **Love and Friendship:** Bless all caring and nurturing signs; all compassion and support; all harmonious relationships in nature and architecture; everything that is connected to or gently touching something else; all signs of cooperation, as in games or work; and all signs of laughter and fun.

✥ **Inner Peace:** Bless all the elements of quietness, calmness, tranquility, and serenity (such as quiet water or still air); all distant views (horizons, stars, the moon); all signs of beauty of sight, sound, or touch; all clear colors and shapes; and all the details of natural or made objects.

✥ **Spiritual Growth:** Bless all indicators of growth, development, and change in nature; the transitions of dawn and twilight; the movement of sun, moon, planets, and stars; the flight of birds in the sky; and the movement of wind and sea.

These ideas are for guidance if you are not used to blessing, but don't be limited by them. Remember that any quality, characteristic, or condition can be blessed (for example, you can bless slender poles and slim animals to encourage weight loss), whether it has existed, presently exists, or exists in your imagination alone.

Personally I have used the power of blessing to heal my body, increase my income, develop many skills, create a deeply loving relationship with my wife and children, and establish a worldwide network of peacemakers working with the *aloha* spirit. It's because it has worked so well for me that I want to share it with you. Please share it with as many others as you can.

Positive Passion

Let's go on with another way to make love practical. The Hawaiian word for this aspect is *kaunu*, and we can translate that as "positive passion." Another meaning is "to make passionate love," but it is also used when you have a passionate interest in something. Positive passion is not like desiring something in the sense of wanting it terribly. That actually sets up a block because what you're also saying to the Universe is "I don't have it and yet I want it." If you focus on something like that enough you can get some limited results, but you're going to create a tremendous amount of stress and tension at the same time. The kind of passion I'm talking about is the same as when you enjoy something tremendously. If you can build up a sense of enthusiastic enjoyment or even passionate enjoyment for the idea of having whatever it is that you want to create in your life, it's going to make it easier to bring it into being.

You probably already have some areas of your life in which things happen easily because you already have the habit pattern and the confidence, and you don't need to put forth much effort to bring it about. Passion, or loving something enough, is a way to break through blocks, overcome fear, and get through doubt. It's not a pushing type of passion and it's not a pulling type of passion; it's a purely enjoyable type of passion. When you are sending out into the world vibrations, thoughts, or feelings of how much you enjoy this thing you are passionate about, then the object of your affection starts coming to you in greater and greater abundance until thinking of the thing is enough to make it happen.

My wife and I have this kind of attitude toward travel. I've traveled since I was two weeks old, and she got to like it after we were together. We both love to travel so much that it's completely natural; we hardly think about it. By lovingly thinking the word "travel," stuff falls into place. She calls it "getting on the escalator" because it feels that effortless. We don't have to sit down and do what some people would, like visualizing, intensifying, and putting energy into it—focusing on every detail. Just loving to travel makes travel easy for us.

It's clear that when you love something enough it becomes abundant and simplified. If it's something you're doing, you become more skillful with less effort. And if you really love dealing with money, that gets easier, too.

I'm going to ask you to do a little exercise just to give you the general process, something you can do more completely on your own.

1. Think of something that you really would like to have in your life—some kind of change, some kind of thing you would like to bring in, some body state, some relationship state, some financial state, whatever kind of thing you would like to have. For right now, forget about trying to bring it into your life. Just have the idea.

2. Find something in your environment that seems to have more energy than other things, such as a light bulb, candle flame, fan, or crystal.

3. Inhale with your attention on the energy source, and exhale with your attention on your head, your heart, your navel, or whatever part of your body you want to energize so you can turn that energy into passion.

4. With your imagination, as much as you want to and as much as you can, enjoy the idea of what it would be like if your want were actually true and real for you right now. Let yourself feel and dwell on how good that would be; let that kind of feeling flow. Just enjoy the idea of it. If a fear or a doubt comes up to mind, grab hold of it, toss it out, and say, "Hey, I'll deal with you later. Right now, let's just enjoy!" Build up this feeling as strongly as you can.

5. When you have reached the peak of what you can do in this session, stop, let go of it, and relax. Do it again when you have the time.

Sometimes in doing this exercise, you may find that you have to do a little more clarifying of what it is you really want.

Remember, the idea is to focus on what you want, not on what you don't want. Enjoy the process as best you can—the good, positive feelings of it—and tell yourself, even if this is the beginning kind of training and even if it's not completely true yet, "Hey, well, I *really* love this! I really love it. This is what I really love to be, to do, to have. Oh, how I love it!" Words can help focus and shape the imagination and intensify the experience.

Some people may be a little uncomfortable doing an experiment like this because they are so used to holding in their passion, or trying not to feel it. Part of this can come from a fear of disappointment, but it might also come from family training. If that's your case, take some time to think about it, and maybe practice it a little by small steps if you want to.

Of all the things we can talk about in terms of intensifying energy, nothing is more powerful than the love motivation. *Nothing.* You can stuff your house full of crystals or you can practice rituals given to you by the most powerful wizard in the world, and you won't get as great an effect as you will from an enthusiastic passion for something you love. Anything else is only helpful at best.

8

Extending Your Influence

****

Ukuliʻi ka pua, onaona i ka maʻu
Tiny is the flower, yet it scents the grasses around it

The quotation above is a proverb from Hawaiian tradition. In English we would call it the "ripple effect." In French it would be *tache dʻhuile,* or "drop of oil." The concept has been recognized all over the world, but somehow the Hawaiian is more poetic and three-dimensional. It says that small things can have large effects. A modern equivalent is chaos theory, which, as we've already discussed in meteorological terms, says that a butterfly flapping its wings in Japan can cause tornadoes in Texas.

Another concept from Hawaii and the most powerful idea in its tradition—one that has spread its influence around the world, meeting and merging with its counterparts in other cultures—is the simple idea of what we have already called "the aloha spirit." Usually translated as "love," it includes the ideas of friendship, acceptance, compassion, mercy, gratitude, assistance, and cooperation. So we say people show *aloha* when they greet you warmly, when they give you a smile, when they help you out if you are in need, when they remember to thank you for a favor, when they act like a friend, when they forgive wrongs done to them. *Aloha* has a sexual side, too, but it always implies a loving sexuality. The association between flowers and love is more than coincidental, since flowers are actually the sexual organs of plants.

It is obvious that the ideas and actions behind *aloha* are not exclusive to Hawaii, and that is the point. Flowers grow in other places besides the Hawaiian Islands. These flowers of love grow wild, and it is wonderful to encounter them by surprise. However, they can also be cultivated and shared more abundantly. Just as we raise flowers with the conscious intent to distribute them as widely as we can, so can we cultivate the practice of love for wider distribution.

Every week during the twenty years that I lived on Kauai, I held "talk story" sessions sponsored by Aloha International where we discussed the philosophy, culture, and traditions of the islands. Before the group got too big, I used to start each session by having participants share their name, where they were from, and some good thing that had happened to them recently. First-time attendees often found it difficult to think of something good because our society subtly encourages us to instead share things that are going wrong. So part of the purpose of this was to get people to think more positively for their own benefit. The most important purpose, however, was experiencing the positive effect it had on everyone else present. It was amazing and, in a way, awesome, to watch everyone's face light up when one person mentioned a simple event, such as seeing a rainbow or a whale, or their pleasure at hosting a visiting friend from the mainland. When an event is shared verbally, listeners replicate it in their own mind and respond to it with their own degree of good feeling. One person's rainbow suddenly becomes a rainbow experienced by twenty-five or more. One solitary, ordinary event increases the pleasure and energy of the whole group. At the end of such a sharing, everyone is high.

The idea behind the tiny flower is that it doesn't really matter how small you are, whether in size or numbers. It doesn't matter how much you know, how skilled you are, or how much education or credentials you have. What really matters is how you affect the world around you.

You are like a tiny flower, and everything you do affects your world. When you smile, others feel better, even when they don't acknowledge it or you aren't aware of them. Haven't you ever smiled in response to seeing two other people smile at each other? Or laughed quietly along with a laughing child? When you help one person, many others feel uplifted. Those others might be some who have benefited from the help, some who have seen the help, some who have heard about the help, or some who have responded in a positive way to the good feelings of those who were helped. Each time you act with loving intent, you are sowing seeds for the growth of others in ways you may never see and among those you may never know. Like the perfume of a tiny flower, the effects of your actions spread far beyond the area of your immediate perceptions.

In relation to governments, big business, and organized religions, an individual person is still a tiny flower. Yet individuals doing simple things that they believe in can change the behavior of multitudes. Consider the following stories.

In the mid-1930s, clothing manufacturers in Honolulu decided that they wanted to make a uniquely Hawaiian type of cloth. Artist Elsie Das was commissioned by Watumull's East India Store in Honolulu to create fifteen floral designs that were sent to Japan to be hand-printed on silk and then made into shirts back in Hawaii. Thus, "*aloha* shirts" were born and grew to be popularized on every continent in the world ever since.

The Merrie Monarch Festival, a kind of international Olympics of *hula*, can be traced back to a Hilo festival on the island of Hawaii, which was sponsored by the County Council and the Chamber of Commerce. It didn't really become a *hula* festival until 1969, however, when chairwoman Dottie Thompson got together with *hula* master George Naope and former government official Albert Nahalea to turn it into a true festival of *hula*. Since then it has been the inspiration for the revival of traditional styles of *hula* as a vital part of Hawaiian culture as well as for the formation of *hula* troupes all over the globe. Today there are over eight hundred hula troupes in Japan alone, and American, German, and Polish dancers from the *halau* of Aloha International were invited to perform for the opening of a bridge between Germany and Poland.

And remember Duke Kahanamoku, who single-handedly introduced the world to Hawaiian surfing, which has now become an Olympic sport and, as of 2006, an $11 billion retail and manufacturing industry?

I could name a lot of other individuals whom we now consider outstanding who have had a great deal of influence in various fields, but the point is that they all started out as tiny flowers without much apparent influence at all. Still, everything they said, everything they did, and everything they thought, was felt and reacted to by others.

"Everything they thought" is what I just said. It is easy to acknowledge the influence of words and things we can see, and it is even easier to acknowledge the influence of charisma or emotions on people nearby. If you have a spiritual background, you can probably acknowledge the influence of prayer as well. In my tradition of Huna, though, we consider every thought to be a prayer. In other words, we are telepathic beings, constantly telepathizing in active and passive modes. We respond to the thoughts of others, and they respond to ours. Contrary to popular fears, no one can control the thoughts of another. But, like the perfume of a tiny flower, we can *influence*. If the perfume smells good, the response will be good. If the smell is bad, the response will be bad. It is only natural that our thoughts can be reflected, or even amplified, in the events of the world around us.

It's almost scary to think that every thought you think is reaching out to touch and modify the world to some degree. And when I say "the world," I don't just mean the people in it; I'm referring to all the plants, animals, elements, and objects as well. It can be even scarier when you remember all the mean things you've thought; all the angry, fearful, vengeful, frightening thoughts you've had from time to time. Have they been having an effect on the world? According to Huna, *yes*. They might do nothing more than nudge a molecule or an electron, or they might add their impetus to ongoing events. But they certainly *do* have an effect.

However, Huna also says that the nature of the Universe is love. And love is the urge toward growth—a desire to increase awareness, skills, and happiness. The whole Universe, and every individual entity within it, is moving toward greater and greater love. This means that anything contrary to love has to go against that movement, like a rock rolling uphill. Under certain natural circumstances, rocks can move against gravity, but it takes a tremendous amount of energy to do that. Human beings, joining their individual energies and ideas, have devised machines to move rocks and other objects against gravity in small amounts for relatively short distances, but the output of energy and effort is considerable. In a similar way, any influences contrary to love require tremendous energy to have any effect.

"Hold on, now!" someone may say. "What about all the evil effects in the world? What about wars, disease, cruelty, and pollution? It seems so easy for these things to happen." The only reason it seems easy for such things to occur is that there already exists a tremendous amount of energy moving in those directions. That energy comes from all the thoughts of fear and anger from all kinds of people all around the planet. In spite of this, love and its effects continue on a far grander scale than any unloving energies. In fact, the bad stuff seems so terrible because it occurs on a background of love so immense that we barely acknowledge it. But individually, when you think angrily or fearfully, you connect to the existing energy of anger and fear, and it amplifies your thoughts' effects while you add your bit to its existence.

Before you cringe and crumble in guilt, it will be helpful to know that you can do something about this. Because love's momentum is so much greater than any contrary force, loving thoughts connect you to that positive power, which also amplifies the effects of your thoughts. In addition, your loving thoughts will neutralize the effects of previous fearful or angry thoughts, the same way that gravity pulling down a wall will neutralize all the energy it took to put it up. On the other hand, thoughts of fear and anger do not neutralize loving thoughts any more than putting up a wall neutralizes the effects of gravity.

Let's talk about loving thoughts: what exactly are they? Any thought that encourages a growth in awareness, skills, or happiness is a loving thought. A positive affirmation can be called a loving thought. A prayer to any form of God for the good of yourself or another is a loving thought. A loving thought can be a mental compliment to a friend or stranger, appreciation for the beauty of a sunrise or sunset, gratitude for a gift, or forgiveness for a hurt. The desire for peace, hope for a better future, or creative visualizations for success and prosperity can be loving thoughts. Any thought in the direction of goodness is a loving one.

What we really need now are more consciously loving thoughts. To return to our flower, most people think that flowers just happen to smell good. In reality, flowers emit their perfume on purpose, influencing specific animals to come and help them pollinate each other. In return for this favor, the flowers provide nectar as a reward—the only purpose that this liquid serves. Not only do flowers emit their perfume on purpose, they also time their emissions to coincide with the natural activities of the animals they wish to influence. The next time you stop to smell the flowers, pay attention to the time of day. Some flowers give off most of their perfume in the morning, some in the afternoon, and some at night. If you smell them at other times, the perfume is weak or nonexistent. It's as if the flowers have more influence when their intention is more conscious.

As a tiny metaphorical flower yourself, your consciously intended thoughts are more powerful than the ones that just happen by, so to speak. More than that, I'm suggesting that the thoughts you think with the specific intent to influence are even more powerful. Beyond that, your most powerful thoughts are those that consciously seek to amplify any inclinations toward goodness that are already out there.

For instance, this first thought is far less effective than the second: (1)"May those greedy developers in South America be prevented from burning down any more of the rainforests"; and (2) "May all those who want to maintain and protect the rainforests have more courage, confidence, and success." In the first case, you are pitting your mental energy against something, while in the second, you are adding it to a growing trend. Likewise, for your own personal health, it is more powerful to think

"My health is increasing" than "I'm getting rid of my illness" because the natural tendency of your body is toward health and not away from illness. Your body doesn't get rid of illness. When it is free enough to do so, it absorbs, transforms, or expels those things that interfere with health. That's quite a different process.

If one tiny flower can scent the grasses around it, then the scent of a million tiny flowers may be carried by the wind to the far corners of the world. Those of us who are praying, blessing, thinking, and acting with the spirit of love in our daily lives are already beginning to have an influence, subtle but growing, in a number of countries, because of the very nature of our focus and because we are a tiny flower among thousands of tiny flowers all emitting the same perfume—the essence of loving power and powerful love.

With almost no resources and very few numbers, we are affecting a whole lot of people for the better. We have barely begun, but we have begun. The world is changing rapidly all around us, and it is changing as a result of inner forces and not outer ones. People in far distant corners of the world are inhaling the fragrance of our tiny flowers and doing things once thought impossible.

Whenever the senseless violence, epidemics, tragedies, and pollution of the world seem overwhelming, open your eyes a little wider and see the increasing good that many individual blooms are creating. Reflect for a while on those who are helping children in other countries to live better and healthier lives; whose inventiveness is increasing communication among all people; who are devising more ways to heal minds and bodies; who are negotiating for peace and understanding between enemies; who are not only keeping an eye on businesses and governments to protect the environment but who are also developing new ways to cooperate with

nature rather than exploit her. Give some appreciation, too, to
the tremendous increase in the number of comedians making
us laugh and to the very existence of a comedy channel on
television, however variable the content might be. All over the
world, in every country, there are people working hard to
make things better. And every positive thought we can have
about them helps them.

It is good to participate in grand causes and to carry out
great projects, but it is not the only way to get things done.
Practicing the *aloha* spirit in your daily life is another valid way.
One of the most encouraging and exciting things I've seen is
the growth of interest in a radical concept exemplified by the
phrase, "Practice random acts of kindness and senseless
beauty." We are so used to thinking in terms of fulfilling needs
that the idea of *just doing* good things randomly—for the fun of
it—is really radical. It jolts us out of old thinking patterns and
inspires us to leave quarters in pay phones or on top of newspaper boxes, to include a thank you note with your bill to the
electric company, to give a gift to an unsuspecting someone, to
pull weeds or pick up litter when no one has asked you to. It's
fun to do these things for strangers but more daring to do it
within your own family. Some people promoting this are using
the term "spiritual guerrillas," which is catchy. But I don't think
we need the warrior connection. I prefer "friendly gremlins."

If you wish to practice more telepathic love, this is an easy
exercise you can do in a comfortable place outside or in a place
where you can look outside. The only prerequisite is that you
do it with your eyes open and in contact with your environment; it really doesn't matter whether you are lying down, sitting, standing, or walking around.

1. Imagine that you are a flower getting ready to send out
   your perfume. Pick a favorite flower and/or your favorite

aroma. If you have the actual aroma at hand, it can aid your imagination.

2. Take a moment to decide who or what you want to send your perfume to and for what purpose. You could send it to a member of your family or a friend, to a group or organization carrying out a task you believe in, or even to groups of plants or animals. Feel that your perfume will give them the strength and the energy to do something of benefit to themselves or to someone or something else.

3. Finally, send your perfume out into the air and imagine that it is going where you want it to go, doing what you want it to do. You can end by affirming this as a fact in your own way.

The ancient Hawaiians often used flowers as poetic symbols for people. As another Hawaiian proverb states,

Mohala i ka wai ka maka o ka pua
Unfolded by the water are the faces of the flowers

People thrive when conditions are good. As more and more tiny flowers gather together to spread their loving influence, we will be helping to create those positive conditions.

9

The Mystery of Money

J kani no ka 'alae i ka wai
A mudhen calls out because it has water
(A prosperous person speaks with authority)

*M*ake sure you have a good grip on this book and buckle up your seatbelt if you have one, because we're going to talk about one of the most difficult subjects there is to talk about: the powerful form of *mana* called "money."

Prosperity, wealth, success, and abundance are all very fine words, but they don't impress your *Ku*. Many people don't know that the subconscious is very literal and practical. In other words, it does not understand abstract concepts. Prosperity, for example, is a vague, nonphysical term; it means a lot of good things. That's not specific enough for the subconscious, though. Anything that is flourishing or thriving can be called prosperous, including ants and weeds. As for abundance, you can have an abundance of lack, you can have an abundance of bills, you can have an abundance of problems. Abundance can mean anything at all to the subconscious. Success is a relative term, too—successful at *what*? You can be just as successful at failing as you are at winning, for example. So when we speak to the subconscious, when we try to program it, we must be specific to get the best results—not detailed, necessarily; just specific.

So let's be specific and talk in terms of money. In this chapter I'll teach you how to start feeling good about money so you can bring more of it into your life.

Your Relationship to Money

First of all, your subconscious can either keep money away by attracting you to circumstances that lead you away from it, or it can keep money from staying in your pockets by helping you to find excuses for giving it away or losing it as quickly as you get it. What you want, I'm assuming, is to get money in abundance. One of the first steps in this project is to learn to be comfortable with money.

It's amazing how many people have strong reactions against that word *money* no matter what the language. So let's try something and see what your reactions are right now.

1. Relax your body, close your eyes, and become aware of your body.
2. Now, do a little money chant. That is, chant the word *money* four times and then three times, and repeat this a few times in the pattern below:

> Money, money, money, money,
> money, money, money.
> Money, money, money, money,
> money, money, money.
> Money, money, money, money,
> money, money, money.

> Money, money, money, money,
> money, money, money.

3. Next, check in with your body. What were your physical reactions to this chant?

Later you can try this a little longer if you like, but for now, how do you feel? What did the exercise do to you? Did you feel squirmy sensations? Did you feel tingling? Was it a positive or negative feeling? Did your throat tighten up, or did you get a pain anywhere? Did memories associated with the experience emerge? Did you see any pictures?

Your reactions will give you clues as to your relationship with money, and if it's been a problem, you may begin to get an idea of why money has eluded you. If you had a strong reaction of any kind, then you have some strong beliefs about money. For example, if you don't have money right now in your life, then those strong reactions and those beliefs are part of the reason that you don't have money. If you had positive reactions, then that's a good sign for future progress in this area. If you had no reactions, then you either already have all the money you want or you are in dire need of more appreciation for it if you don't.

Let's look at what we can call the "anti-money programming" that many of us have been subjected to all our lives.

How often have you heard the idea that money is the root of all evil? It's probably been played over and over and over again throughout your life. And you've probably been told that this statement comes from the Bible. That's actually not true. The exact phrase in the Bible is "For the love of money is the root of all evil," and it is attributed to Paul in his first letter to Timothy, chapter 6, verse 10. In this context, he is condemning those who put the love of money above their love of God or the doing of good works. He doesn't condemn money itself, and he doesn't condemn rich people as such.

Another idea heard frequently is that money is power and power corrupts. This is a misquote from a statement made by an Englishman named Lord Acton, who was writing specifically about politics in the nineteenth century. He actually said, "Power tends to corrupt, and absolute power corrupts absolutely." You would do well to think about that if you are going to be a politician, but the statement wasn't made about money.

How often have you heard about the "idle rich" or heard someone say they want to be "filthy rich"? What about the idea that wealthy people are ruthless or that you have to be mean and a cheat and a crook in order to be wealthy? If you're a nice, average person who doesn't want to be idle, filthy, or evil, and you've been told all your life that money causes these things, why on earth would you want to have a lot of money?

If this message sounds familiar, then quite unconsciously you will find yourself engaged in certain situations and behavioral patterns in order to avoid getting a lot of money. If you don't have a lot of money in your life, it's more than likely because you don't think you should. And I'm not talking about conscious belief; I'm talking about something that is lodged in your subconscious. Once you know it's there, you can work to get it out.

Perhaps you had a religious upbringing that idealized poverty, preached the difficulty of the rich getting to Heaven, talked about karma, or talked about God's will. If you accept the idea that it is God's will that you be poor, or that it's your unchangeable karma, then you might as well not read this chapter. But I'm telling you that this is *not* so. All through the Bible, God's message was of abundance, of all the good things coming to God's children. God gave the great flocks and fields and riches to Abraham, and God also gave them to Jacob. Jesus, though he wandered, never lacked for food and lodging unless he did it voluntarily. And even Jesus spoke of the greatness and the riches that God gives. All throughout the Bible, you will find this to be true. As for karma, it is actually a Sanskrit word meaning "action" and, by extension, "reaction." By itself, karma does not mean cause and effect over time. Action and reaction always take place in the present moment, and if you are willing to accept that in order to change your karma, then you're on your way to prosperity.

This whole earth is filled with the potential for abundance for *you* if you will accept it—*if* you will accept it.

How Money Works

It is sad that so few people understand or appreciate what money really is. This lack of knowledge contributes a great deal to the lack of money.

In one of my workshops, I demonstrate the common misconception that money has power by setting a bill of large denomination on a table and demanding that it do something, *anything*. Of course, nothing happens because money only has the power that human beings give to it.

The most important thing to understand is that money is merely a means of exchange for goods and services. That's it; that's all. And it is not only the stamped coins and printed bills that most people use today. It is *anything* that is used as a medium of exchange for goods and services.

Barter is a different kind of exchange, one that some believe is better and purer than a money exchange. In barter, you give me a massage and I teach you a skill; or I give you a banana and you give me an apple. It is a direct exchange of goods and services, and it works quite well—as long as I want your massage or you want my banana. When that's not the case, the system breaks down. In my early days of giving courses, I used to trade crystals for my teaching until I realized the crystals were not paying for my travel and lodging. After that, I told those people to sell the crystals and then come to my courses.

Barter is an ancient concept, and so is money. In Old Hawaii, the islands were divided into pie-shaped districts called *ahupua'a* that ran from the sea to the mountains. Each district was both a political and economic unit, designed to be as self-sufficient as possible. The people on the coast would trade fish and vegetables with the people of the uplands for fruit and lumber. That worked well until someone from one district wanted something special from another district, like a fine wood carving or the well-made stone tool of a highly skilled craftsman. Those people didn't want fish or vegetables or fruit or lumber because they already had them available. But they were willing to take an alternative item with more universal trade and investment appeal. A number of different things were used for this, but the most common was a bundle of *tapa*, a type of cloth made from tree bark that was used to make a lot of different things, including clothing, blankets, wrapping, candle wicks, and oakum, for caulking the seams in boats and ships. Because of its versatility, *tapa* became one of the most common forms of money in Old Hawaii, with higher quality *tapa* traded for more valuable things. It was barter when it was traded directly for some kind of goods and services, and money when it was traded indirectly, that is, held until it could be traded for something else.

On the Micronesian island of Yap in the Western Pacific they use three kinds of money, two of them from ancient times and one from modern times. The most unusual kind of money is what looks like a round wheel of coral or crystalline calcite, about four to eight inches thick (10 to 20 cm) with a hole in the center. The diameter could range from a couple of feet across to as much as twelve feet. I saw a "bank" there, which consisted of a hut with a fenced yard full of various sized wheels belonging to different community members. These wheels are only used to buy and sell real estate, and you can't own property on Yap without a wheel being either in a bank or displayed on the property. The second type of money, a special shell, was used for purchasing a bride; and the third type, the U.S. dollar, was used for buying beer.

In ancient Africa the most common form of money was the cowrie shell, although gold was used to some extent. All around the world, different societies and cultures have used something of value to them for money. And this leads us to the second most important thing to understand about money: its value as money is always arbitrary.

There is a big difference between intrinsic value and perceived value. For instance, gold has intrinsic value as jewelry or decoration because it's shiny, it doesn't tarnish, and it mixes well with other metals to make it more durable. It also has use in some conditions for electrical connections because it doesn't tarnish, but that is offset by the fact that is not a very good conductor. However, its value as a symbol of success, as an amulet to ward off evil, and especially as a form of money is imaginary—purely a product of someone's arbitrary decision and others' agreement with that decision. Gold is fairly rare, but being rare doesn't automatically make it valuable. I have a rock from a place called Richat in the deep Sahara that has some unusual physical properties. It is extremely rare since these rocks exist only in that area and nowhere else in the world. Unfortunately, no one wants to buy it or use it for trade, and so it has no value despite its rarity.

It used to be a very popular thing among nations to use the so-called "gold standard," meaning that the currency they printed and minted was "backed" by gold. The idea of real, physical gold sitting somewhere was supposed to make people feel more secure about the currency. Finally, someone realized that this was not only arbitrary, since it was based on a made-up value, but it was also inconvenient, as it was impossible to keep up with the amounts of money required in a growing modern world. Now, in the United States at least, money is not backed by anything tangible at all. It is backed by the Gross National Product, a phrase meaning the expected value of the total production of Americans in a given year, and that's about as intangible as it's possible to get.

So the currency you use for money is based on whatever value that you and other people believe it has. The actual paper and metal has very little intrinsic value, and no matter how pretty your money is, the people of another country may not think it has any value at all. The paper money of the United States is not very pretty at all, yet it is considered one of the most valuable currencies in the world. On the other hand, I have some beautiful five shilling notes from the Republic of Biafra that I would find hard to give away. I do have a reason for putting such emphasis on this, which will be clear in the next section.

Increasing Your Value

The value of the money in your pocket depends on how valuable it is to the people you want to buy something from. In exactly the same way, the financial value of your goods and services depends on how valuable they are to the people you want to get money from. And that depends much more on their perception of you than it does on the intrinsic value of your goods and services.

While researching different styles of massage, I took a course for getting licensed as a massage therapist in Los Angeles. It was a good course with good instructors, and along with twenty other people, I learned how to do the standard "Esalen-type" massage that was required for the license. Although it was not my intention to earn a living at it, that was the purpose for all the others who were there.

Midway through the course, we were encouraged to start charging for massages, and shortly before the end of the course, the main instructor gathered us together to ask what people had been charging. Remember, everyone in the class was doing the same massage. Not counting my practice of charging nothing, the lowest price charged for an hour's massage, by a sweet, shy young woman, was $10, and the highest price charged for an hour's massage, by a husky, confident young man, was $100. Most of the others ranged around $35— all for the same massage!

The difference had nothing to do with the intrinsic value of the massage. The only difference was in the perceived value of the therapist. And what was the source of that perception? The therapist.

To increase your value in the eyes of yourself and others, it's helpful to be aware of the factors that contribute to your personal value. Here are some things that help to influence how other people perceive you:

1. **Personal energy:** This is another way of describing charisma, which we discussed in chapter 6. It is a special personal quality that gives a person influence over others. And I've told you the benefits and process for this else-where. Increasing your charisma naturally increases your value.

2. **Personal perception:** This is how you think about your-self, especially in the presence of others. Your own attitude toward yourself affects other people in many ways. There is a telepathic aspect to this, of course, but you can ignore

that if you want to because there are other aspects as well. The thoughts and feelings you have about yourself are displayed to other people in your posture; in the way you dress; in the way you speak about yourself and your work; in subtle changes of skin tone and muscle tension that they notice subconsciously; and even in your emission of pheromones, which you can think of as extremely subtle aromas that powerfully affect people's feelings about you.

3. **Personal expectations:** This is how you think about the other people around you, including clients and customers as well as friends and relatives. More specifically, it is about the expectations you have for their behavior and your reactions when those expectations are met, or not met. Some of the aspects listed above operate here, as well.

4. **Personal behavior:** This could cover a lot of things, but I will focus on one thing in particular: how you behave toward people related in any way to your income. This includes clients and customers, naturally, but also suppliers, creditors, and contacts. The more that your behavior makes them feel good, the more money they will help you to make.

Here are some more things to think about doing in order to increase your value:

Self-Esteem

You can't have too much self-esteem. I'm not talking about arrogance, which is a cover-up for low self-esteem; or comparing yourself to anyone else, which is a waste of time. I'm talking about increasing your own value in your own eyes. There are two steps involved in doing this. The order is not important, and they can even be done at the same time.

1. Make an arbitrary decision—not based on "facts" or memories or what anyone else has ever told you—that you as a person, and whatever you have to offer in exchange for money, are extremely valuable and useful to the world. Practice thinking this way for one minute, then five minutes, then an hour, then a day.
2. Make another decision not to doubt the above decision, and practice that in the same way.

Self-Confidence

You can't have too much self-confidence, either. Oh, I know that there are people who will immediately jump on this and say that there's great danger in trying to do something that you really can't do, or that too much self-confidence will blind you to what's really happening. Well, I'm not talking about stupidity or blindness. Self-confidence is about knowing what you know and knowing what you need to know. It's about being aware of what's happening and trusting yourself to be able to deal with it in the best way you know how. It's also about having the confidence to ask for help, as well as expecting things to work out for the best after you've done everything you can. And finally, it's about trusting that you've done everything you can. There are two steps for developing self-confidence, too:

1. Trust what you know how to do, and always seek to improve what you know how to do, physically and mentally.
2. Never ever doubt yourself unless you have a solution that will remove the doubt. Practice these steps as you did for self-esteem.

Added Benefit

In the minds of most people, the benefits of good treatment are more valuable than specific goods or services, or even money itself. Many people, myself included, will pay more for a product or a service that might be cheaper elsewhere if it is accompanied by better treatment.

"Good treatment," or "better treatment," refers to the manner in which goods or services are provided, the addition of extra goods or services not related to the ones paid for, and the follow-up assistance when there is a problem.

The last time I bought a car, I was in a position to make my choice from a number of different automobile dealers. All of the cars of the type I wanted were in the same price range and had pretty much the same features. The one I finally bought was a make I hadn't owned since I was a teenager, and it was from a dealer I had never bought from before. The price was good, but I was more influenced by the fact that the dealer gave me extra features without extra cost, a free car wash whenever I wanted one, and very courteous treatment whenever I needed help. The price and quality of the vehicle were important factors, but the added benefits are the reasons I bought that particular car.

I work on my computer a lot, and I have a large number of internet service providers to choose from, many of whom throw in lots of added benefits in the form of extra features. However, the one I stayed with for years was a small company with no extra features or price breaks. But I could speak to a live person when I called, the person who answered always recognized my name, and when I needed help the person always took the time with immediacy, patience, and skill. I finally did change to another company that provided a better connection with equally good service.

Added benefits can take the form of extra features and extra services, but for many people nothing beats the value of friendliness, courtesy, and personal assistance. The human touch that shows respect cannot be evaluated in terms of money, and yet it can help you make more money than you ever could without it.

Tithing

A discussion about money wouldn't be complete without mentioning the greatly misunderstood practice of tithing.

The word *tithing* originally came from an Old English system of dividing a community into groups of ten men who were legally responsible for each other's behavior. Later, the words *tithing* and *tithe* came to mean a tenth part of anything. That's why it was used to translate the concept of the religious tax imposed on the early Hebrews to support their priesthood, which consisted of a tenth part of their crops or herds. Very probably it was also related to the agricultural practice of putting aside a portion of one's crop or herd for seeding or breeding to ensure future supplies for survival.

In modern times, the concept has undergone some transformation. It is still used by many religious groups as a basis for supporting their organizations, but it is also used by many people as a basis for investments—a sort of "seeding and breeding" with money. Then there are those who see it as a good practice for supporting any source of inspiration, spirituality, or good works that are important to you.

Another belief that has grown up around tithing is that it's a good way to increase your financial prosperity. That's true but not in the way that many people think.

A prevailing metaphysical belief about tithing is that by giving 10 percent of your income to something good, the Universe will magically ensure that you will get 100 percent back. The fact that it seems to work sometimes makes this belief stronger. The fact that it fails more often is mostly ignored.

It would be nice if the Universe paid you back ten times over for giving away only 10 percent of your income. We could solve the poverty issue in no time. Unfortunately, the Universe is not some great slot machine geared in your favor; it doesn't work that way. The Universe gives back exactly what you put into it, and the currency it deals in consists of beliefs and expectations. The upside is that the Universe gives back exactly what you put into it, and the currency it deals in consists of beliefs and expectations. (Don't write the publisher; that was not a typographic error. I meant what I just wrote.)

When tithing does work to increase your financial prosperity—that is, when you give some money away and you get more back—it works for two reasons. One is that, to the degree that you really believe without a doubt that you will get more back, the Universe will accommodate that belief by providing means to bring that about. The second reason is that if you give money away *and that increases your feeling of prosperity*, then the Universe will accommodate that feeling by providing means to increase your prosperity to the level of your new feeling.

Simply put, if you tithe (or give any portion) with the hope that the Universe will pay you back because it is supposed to, then you won't get very good results. If you tithe with the unqualified expectation that it will work, then you will receive according to your expectations. If you tithe and it makes you feel more prosperous, you will receive according to the strength of your feeling.

Tithing is good for the people you tithe to; of that there is no doubt. If that's the only reason you tithe, your benefits may or may not be financial, but they will be real.

Therefore, from a Huna point of view,

- ✥ Money is what you think it is.
- ✥ Money is unlimited because you can have as much as you believe you can.
- ✥ Prosperity increases according to your expectations.
- ✥ If you want more money, start doing what it takes right now.

✦ The more you love what you do and the more you appreciate money, the more you'll make.

✦ The power to prosper comes from you.

✦ And finally, if one way of making more money doesn't work, either change yourself or change what you're doing.

10

The Restaurant of the Universe

Ana 'oia i ka hopena
Truth is measured by results

We live in a world of possibilities and probabilities, and knowing the difference is essential to increasing success and prosperity in the shortest time possible.

A possibility is anything that might happen according to the nature of the Universe. Based on the second principle ("There are no limits"), Huna teaching says that the Universe is infinite. Therefore, anything is possible.

A probability is anything that is likely to result according to the constraints of local limitations. In the life we are living right now, anything may be possible but not everything is *probable*. The distinction is important. I like to explain it by saying that anything is possible if you can figure out how to do it.

Probabilities come out of patterns. It's almost like planting a seed, for a particular seed is a pattern for a particular kind of plant. When you plant that seed, you get a probable plant—a plant most likely to come out of that seed. Normally, you do not get an apple tree when you plant an acorn. Within the range of all kinds of probable possibilities related to that acorn, one is that a squirrel might dig it up before it grows; one is that it might grow only so high and a deer might eat the young shoot; one is that it might grow a little taller and somebody will break it down for a bit of kindling; one is that it might grow into a giant oak; and so on. There are all kinds of probabilities within the potential of that acorn, but all of them stem out of that acorn. Thus, probabilities of any kind have to come out of seeds that are planted, whether physical or not. The seeds, as far as you are concerned with your future experience, are your patterns of thought and behavior that are based on those thoughts.

The Game Metaphor

One of my favorite ways of explaining this further is to use the metaphor of a game like *konane*, a Hawaiian game similar to checkers. In this game, you use a board made up of an even number of rows and columns of small pits. All the pits are filled alternately with pieces of black lava or white coral. Two people play the game, one taking the coral and the other the lava rock. At the beginning, a white piece and a black piece are removed from the center of the board. The object of the game is to remove the other player's pieces by jumping over them with your pieces in such a way as to be able to make the last move. In playing the game, you may not jump your own pieces, but you can jump in any direction as many times as possible, and you can start your turn with any moveable piece. The winner, as indicated above, is the one who can make the last move.

However, since the Universe is infinite and anything is possible, there is nothing really stopping you from removing the other player's pieces immediately, or from distracting your opponent and stealing some of his pieces while he isn't looking, or from adding more of your black pieces into the empty pits when you feel like it. You could do that, of course, but then you wouldn't be playing *konane*. If you want to play a particular game, you have to play within the rules—both the constraining rules and the playing rules.

Life as we know it is much like a game. The constraining rules, like the board and the number of pits in *konane*, are things like time, space, gravity, and electromagnetism. The ideas we have *about* those things, as well as about everything else in life, are the playing rules. So we can play *konane* all our life, or we can change the playing rules and play a different game on the same board. Applying Huna principles, with a healthy dash of shamanistic thinking thrown in, is like using the same board with a shifted set of playing rules (as well as altered shapes and names for the pieces) and finding yourself playing the ancient Arabic game of *Quirkat*. By changing some of the rules, we have opened up a vastly greater number of possibilities and probabilities in the same space and time context.

The Restaurant Metaphor

My wife thinks the game metaphor is too intellectual. As a professional dietitian, she prefers to think of the Universe as a great big restaurant, with a virtually infinite menu, an extremely versatile chef, and a very attentive waiter. You can have anything on the menu, but there are two conditions:

1. It has to be available when you want it.
2. You have to give your order to the waiter.

When you walk into a normal restaurant, you can sit at the table until the restaurant closes but you won't get a meal until you tell the waiter what you want. The same is true of the

Restaurant of the Universe (RU). The difference is that as soon as you sit down in the RU, the waiter is automatically going to serve you what you ordered last time, unless you change your order. And if you order something that isn't available, like fruit out of season, the waiter will suggest a substitution, at least until what you want is in stock.

Now, this applies to anything, but in the context of this book, it particularly applies to those things that you want to do, be, or have. In this present moment, the success that you have—your financial success, your material success, or your spiritual success—and the resources that you have to do things with—what your environment is like right now—are all part of a probability that grew out of your past patterns of thinking and behavior. It's not just chance. In the sense of something happening without a cause, that doesn't exist in this Universe.

Your future probabilities are being planted right now by your present thinking and behavior. If you really want to know what your prosperity is going to be like in the future, you don't need a psychic to tell you whether you are going to be rich or not. All you have to do is take a good look at the present, and you will gain a clear sense of what your future successes are going to be like.

Fortunately, the RU menu changes daily, your present moment keeps changing, and you have the ability to change your thinking and behavior anytime. Because of that, you have the ability to plant different seeds or to order a different meal, and therefore, to create a different kind of future. You're never stuck with what you have right now any more than you are "stuck" with having to eat the same thing for breakfast, lunch, and dinner when choice is available.

Another nice thing about the Restaurant of the Universe is that it has a satisfaction guaranteed policy. This means that if you don't like what you get, you can send it back and order something else without offending the chef. Also, if you pay attention, you can take advantage of the special offers that are presented from time to time.

How to Make Changes

The main message here is simple: If you want to change something, you have to change something. If you want to bring another kind of experience into your life, you have to do something to alter your present attitude and behavior so that you will attract this new experience to you. That means planting a new seed, changing the rules, or ordering something else from the menu of life. These are all different ways of trying to describe the experience, and it really doesn't matter which one you choose to go by as long as you get a feeling for the concept.

At some point, existence requires change. There may be things in your life right now that you like and you want to keep. In that case, you might want to keep the same attitudes and behaviors that maintain them. Some things you may just want to modify a little bit. In that case, you would modify a bit of your thinking and behavior. And some things you may want to replace entirely, in which case you must replace entirely your related thinking and behavior in that area. As always, what you've been doing has brought you what you have. If you try to change your experience without changing yourself, you're not going to get results. Something must change inside—some way of believing about yourself, about events, about the world.

Now, how do you make changes? This is the really important part. How do you alter your present situation into one that's happier, more productive, more abundant, more aligned with what you want? There are a number of different ways to do this—and all of them involve change.

Change Your Judgments

Judgments are your decisions about whether something is good or bad. If you are in a particular situation and you call it bad, you're going to be resisting it, fighting it, not wanting it. That in itself is a way of ensuring that it stays there. In resisting it, you are focusing your attention on its present state—and you're keeping it around. If you have a particular kind of salary or job that you repeatedly say is bad—"I don't like it," "I can't stand it," "I hate it"—and you keep thinking along those lines, you're going to be helping yourself to ensure that this condition, or one very much like it, stays in your life simply because you're fighting it so hard. Give up your judgment and become indifferent about it—really and truly indifferent, not just suppressing your feelings—and release the pressure that you've been using to push against it. When you stop resisting, the undesirable circumstance will start changing on its own, which means your experience will start to change as well. Maybe the job will get better, maybe it will become more enjoyable, maybe the pay will increase, or maybe another opportunity will come. All the things that you've been holding back with that negative focus will be released and a cleansing flow will be allowed to take place. So changing your judgments can improve your success when you've been judging something as negative or bad. This goes along with the first principle of Huna: "The world is what you think it is."

Change Your Interpretation

Interpretation is a little different from judgment. It might not be that you decide that something is good or bad but that you decide something has to exist in a particular way.

A person who says, "Well, all I can make is $20,000 a year. That's my limit!" is making his or her own interpretation of what the limit is. A person who says statements such as "I don't have the talent or experience to change jobs, or to improve my situation," "I'm a woman, and I can't get certain types of jobs," "I'm too old for certain types of jobs or for certain kinds of income," "I can never make money," "I can never hold money," or "Money always slips through my fingers" is just making interpretations of reality based on his or her own decisions, not stating facts. And if you are making such interpretations, they'll remain true for you as long as you hold them. One way to change your condition is to change how you are interpreting your present reality. You can look at the whole situation and say, "Hey, what if this weren't true? What if I were to start acting as if it weren't true?" That's one way to get started on the process. Another way is to pretend that this new idea is already true—for example, "Yes, I may not be as young as I once was, but I can switch careers and double my salary." Accomplishing these goals starts with believing they're possible. You are going to have to reinterpret reality. The Huna principle to remember here is that there are no limits (except the ones you invent).

Change Your Expectations

If you are sincerely expecting the worst with all your heart, you will probably get it. Expectations are a fascinating study. Just before the stock market crash of 1929, a man owned a successful restaurant in the southern part of the United States. It served big portions of food, it had signs all up and down the highway to get people to stop, and everybody who came through got great food and great service. The restaurant was doing huge business, and it was expanding. Then the Depression hit. The owner of the restaurant was down in the South and didn't pay any attention to it. His business was going well, he was hiring more people, and people were still stopping while they were traveling.

One day his son came home from college up North and said, "Dad, what are you doing? There's a depression on! Didn't you know the whole economy is falling apart?"

"No, what are you talking about?" asked the restaurant owner.

"The economy's falling apart, and you don't know what that means," said his son. "People are losing their jobs, there's not enough money, supplies are getting low. You can't keep operating like this."

The man was uneducated and figured his son must know what he was talking about, so he started cutting back on his portions, quit hiring so many people, and let go the few employees he thought might be extra. Then he figured, "Those highway signs cost a lot of money to keep up, and if fewer people are coming because of the depression, I won't need them." So he took down some of them. And sure enough, fewer people started coming and business went down. Fewer and fewer people stopped, the place got kind of grubby, and the food got worse until the restaurant just went out of business. As he finally closed the doors, he said, "You're right, son. There is a depression."

It's easy to see in this case how the man's expectations of a particular word's meaning brought about the failure of his business. Depressions, repressions, suppressions and all those other "sions" don't mean anything to somebody who decides not to believe in them. There are areas in the world with severe economic difficulties, and right next to them are areas where you wouldn't know there was anything wrong. You might think it's because they've got a lot of money in those areas, but I suggest you think about why they have a lot of money. It can't be just inheritance because lots of people inherit money and lose it quickly. It can't be just exploitation because a lot of poor people exploit others and a lot of rich people help others. You can invent all kinds of external excuses for differences in wealth or success, but all that will do is make you feel helpless and angry. The real differences come from inside. The people who are not affected by lack are not listening to it, not caring about it, not fighting it, not afraid of it. In other words, they have different expectations. Some of those people probably inhaled those attitudes unconsciously as they grew up, but some of them no doubt worked their way into them. And that's why they've got what they've got and why they're doing what they're doing. Now, since an expectation is also a belief, you have the ability to alter your expectations to pull a different kind of probability into your life. The Huna idea is to focus on what you want and not on what you don't want.

Change Your Focus

When I say change your focus, I'm talking about changing your whole structure of thinking—not just a belief here and there but the whole way you are thinking about something. Looking at it from a completely different point of view is sometimes enough to radically change the probability that you're bringing in. When you're making any of these changes, regardless of the kind of process you're using, it's important to have in mind what you want. This can take the form of setting goals, but it doesn't have to be that formal. You need some indication in your mind of the kind of life you want to be leading. This alone requires a bit of a change because you have to open up yourself to the possibilities. Here, we're not talking about probabilities; we're talking about possibilities, because you have to begin with possibilities. When you start working toward those, they become probabilities.

As a human being, it is imperative to know that you have access to the possibility of achieving anything any other human being has done. It's not necessarily probable, given your own patterns of behavior and thought, but it is possible. Your limitations at the very least are only those of every other human being. The other thing you must do is look at your own talents, abilities, inclinations, and urges with the realization that all of these represent potential futures for you in a successful way. If you really focus any of these abilities or urges, you could realize them. Do you like the idea of having a $400,000 yacht? That's possible because $400,000 yachts do exist. Do you like the idea of living in a mansion overlooking the ocean? That's possible because there are a lot of mansions like that around the world. None of the things that other people do or have are impossible for you to do and have. They all exist. All you have to do is change the probabilities by restructuring the way you think. Here's one method that I call "Detached Attachment":

1. The first step is to become aware of yourself as spirit or as pure consciousness. In more practical terms, this means a realization that you are not your body—you just *have* a body. In the same way, you are not any of the conditions that are in your environment; you are not identified with these things. It's the process of disidentifying with the situation you're in, whatever it happens to be. It is a realization that you are the consciousness who is aware of these things. If you say, "I am broke," for instance, from this point of view that's not really so. As spirit, as awareness, as consciousness, you can't really be broke. If you say, "I am angry," "I am poor," or "I am physically disabled," or whatever you happen to be, it would entail the realization that this isn't really you. This is just a condition that you're aware of, but it isn't you. When you start to disidentify with the situation, a curious feeling starts to arise; I can only describe it as a sense of free floating. And it's amazing how a particular situation's tension just flows right out and flows away when you're not directly involved. You are merely the eye who is aware.

2. The second step consists of focusing on the kind of condition that you want. Let's put these two steps together in terms of money. As pure consciousness or pure awareness,

you don't need any money. What, then, do you need money for? Look around at your life and your environment, and ask, "Who is it that really needs money?" Well, the savings and loan that holds your mortgage needs money, so from this kind of position, you would focus your mind on that savings and loan regularly receiving whatever that payment is every month. From this point of consciousness, you are programming for your savings and loan company. After all, they risk their capital when they put out a loan, and now they want to be paid back. So you focus on them receiving their money as a kind of a service. Make sense? You might think that your children need food and clothing, and they need money to do different things. Great! Focus on them having all the things that they need, and see them in an abundant situation: well-clothed, well-fed, having spending money, and going to school. Then you might say to yourself, "Hey, I need clothes. I can't go around in these rags every day." Wait a second. As pure spirit, as pure consciousness, you don't need clothes—your body does. From this point of detachment, then, it's almost like stepping back and saying, "OK, body. I realize that you need to have clothes and I love you, so I'd like you to have some good clothes." The new focus is on your body having these clothes, having money to spend, or having the different kinds of things that a body needs, realizing all the time that you're not directly involved. You are attached because you care, because you have concern, because you love. But you are also detached because you're not working on yourself. You cannot prosper yourself because your self isn't even physical. You're starting to get the idea of how this focus is taking place. You have stepped back a little bit in a sense, and you are free now because you don't have to be concerned with yourself. You're free to put all this energy, focus, and help out to everything and everybody around you. And there is a tremendous liberation with that whole approach.

3. The third step involves releasing any resistance to what already is. This is what stops people from making these changes in patterns and bringing in new probabilities. They might say, for instance, "Well, OK, right now I'm living in a shack and I want to be living in a mansion," and they keep looking at that shack and getting angry. Or they look at the shack and say, "How is this possible to change? I have this shack here and I want a mansion." They keep getting upset about the contrast between the two. That resistance, that kind of fighting, blocks energy for change. The probability that you are experiencing and living right now is one probability all by itself. What you're going to plant, or attract, or order is a different probability; it has nothing to do with the one you already have. Your current situation does not stand in the way.

4. The fourth step is a simple one: Persist until you have what you want. In other words, just keep doing the other three steps. It's not like you decide to do it once and then forget about it. That's like planting a seed and not watering it, or ordering a meal and leaving the restaurant. What you do instead is keep this attitude of Detached Attachment as you maintain a spirit of service for all the things, places, and people around you. You also keep releasing whatever *is*, letting it be and accepting changes as they come—the way they come—while feeling the freedom to reject near equivalents if they come up. Just keep up the process. As the seventh principle of Huna tells us, "Effectiveness is the measure of truth."

Near Equivalents

Whenever you focus on something, the Universe answers you immediately. But to the degree that you have any fear or doubt, it answers you in near equivalents to what you're asking for. I talked about near equivalents earlier, but I'd like to discuss them in greater depth. For instance, if you ask the Universe for a white Mercedes, you may get a blue Ford instead. That's called a near equivalent. It isn't that you are not supposed to have a white Mercedes, it's just that the strongest current probability, given what's available and how much fear and doubt you have, is a blue Ford.

A friend of mine started a strong money focus for a project he was working on and received an answer from the Universe just a couple hours later. He stopped at his office to pick up some materials that needed to be returned to the person who had left them there. On top of the pile, he noticed a check for quite a bit of money that was not made out to anyone. It was in the realm of his possibility to say, "Well, the Universe gave me this check, and it's a near equivalent," but it was not within his ethical probability. He thanked the Universe anyway, saying, "Nice try, Universe. Let's do it a little differently next time."

Whenever you concentrate on something with a clear focus, you will often receive near equivalents to what you're asking for. They can come in the form of actual, physical things or things that you hear in the news, in the newspaper, on television, or in telephone calls. You may get near equivalents in all kinds of ways, and it's up to you to decide whether you'll accept the ones that come or if you'll keep on working until you get something more to your liking. In the car example, if you were really focusing on a Mercedes, you might have in mind a white Mercedes with a light blue, leather interior. It would be possible, while you are focusing on this for someone to come up and give you the opportunity to have a green Mercedes with a black interior. You could say, "Thanks, Universe. I'll take this!" That would be a near equivalent to what you were asking for, and you could accept the difference. On the other hand, you could say,

"Thanks, Universe, but this isn't the one I wanted. I'm going to keep on working." The third possibility is that you say, "Thanks, Universe! I'll drive this one until you bring the one I want." The Universe doesn't care what you choose. It will bring you the nearest thing available according to your expectations, interpretations, judgment, fear, doubt, and focus.

Someone asked me once whether they could go to a lonely mountain in New England and start focusing on a green-haired, blue-skinned girl to walk by. Of course, if they put enough energy into that and if they stayed there long enough, in some fashion or other, it would happen. If you stop to think about it, even in a practical, physical reality, there are a number of ways in which that could happen. Someone could be making a movie up on the mountain, and one of the people could come by dressed in makeup like that. Maybe a spaceship would land and a blue-haired girl with green skin would appear. Or perhaps, in wandering around the woods, you might come across an old comic book featuring such a girl. There are quite a few possible ways for this kind of thing to happen. The probabilities are kind of low, but with enough focus, some kind of near equivalent would occur.

The point to this chapter is that, with a clear focus, the Universe delivers what you want. In the Restaurant of the Universe there are no limits; it is abundant. What it can provide it will, but it will only provide according to the probable pattern of your focus. There is a very old legend in Hawaii about a magical tree that could produce all kinds of abundance in unlimited quantities—but only for those who could see it.

11

Decision Jitters

Maka'ala ke kanaka kāhea manu
A man who calls birds should always be alert
(Be prepared for opportunity)

*M*y mother once sent me a miniature dartboard for my desktop, complete with miniature darts. On the dartboard itself were various statements like "Work Early," "Work Late," "Do It Now," "Do It Tomorrow," "Take a Vacation." It was designed to help a busy executive make decisions. I got very good at hitting "Take a Vacation" whenever I wanted to, so it really didn't help much. Still, wouldn't it be nice if there were some absolutely sure way to make the right decision all the time? I mean, what if there were something better than tossing a coin, doing a chart, spinning a dial, or throwing a dart. Whoever could come up with something like that could get very rich very quickly.

I'm not holding my breath, however. The problem is that we never have enough information to make a guaranteed right decision every time we need to. We usually end up either patting ourselves on the back for having made the right decision when things turn out well or condemning ourselves for having made the wrong decision when things don't turn out well. The silly part of this is that the decisions themselves were totally unrelated to the way things turned out.

Let's take a closer look at that. If something turns out well and you congratulate yourself on having made the right decision that led to it, then you are also assuming that events are predestined. Many people do assume that making a decision about the future is like choosing a direction at a crossroads: One road will take you to fame and fortune, and the other will take you to failure and grief. All you have to do is pick the right one.

If life were that neat, then all we'd need would be good road maps. And to get those, all we'd need to do would be to make exactly the same decisions that people made who have already reached fame and fortune. After all, that's how real road maps are made. Follow the same route that other people have taken, and you'll get to where you want to go. So why hasn't it been done? Where are the roadmaps to fame and fortune, health and fitness, love and happiness, spirituality and mystical union? If all you have to do is make the right decisions, why is there such confusion and such a vast selection of maps?

I'll tell you why: Moving into the future is not like traveling over the land, where everything pretty much stays in the same place. It's more like traveling over the ocean, where everything is changing all the time. The more knowledge you have and the more skillful you are, the more often you are likely to be successful. But there can be no guarantee that the next trip will be the same, even though you make all the "right" decisions you made before. There are just too many unknowns. If the future were like that we'd have better weather forecasts, no one would bother to bet on races, and everyone would get rich in the stock market.

So what can you do when faced with an important decision? Here's my advice:

1. If you want any possibility of a good result, the first thing to do is give up being afraid to make the decision because you might not get what you want. If you are unwilling to take any risk whatsoever, you might as well lie down and die right now. (But then how do you know if that would be a good decision?) And how would you know if not making a decision would be a good decision?

2. Be prepared to modify your decision whenever that seems to be a good idea. To go back to the marine analogy, you might start your voyage under full sail, but if the weather changes, it might be wise to modify your sails as well.

3. Increase your knowledge and skill as much as you can, while not expecting to be all-wise or perfect. By the time you know everything there is to know and are so skilled you are never in error, any reason for making the decision will be long gone.

4. The most important thing you can do comes after you make the decision: Keep your mind on what you want and not on what you don't want. I would venture to say that out of all the things we have any control over (and they are few, indeed), this is the one that has the most influence over how well something turns out. The decision to set sail is over in a moment. Then comes the sailing, and that plays a far more important role in whether or not the trip is successful. Keep your mind on the goal, and give as little attention as possible to what's in the way. When that cannot be avoided, keep your mind on the solutions and ignore the problems to the best of your ability.

Remember, it isn't the map that gets you where you want to go; it's what you do after you read it.

Decisions and Values

One day I found myself wondering why we celebrate New Year's Day on January 1. After all, what's the point? Nothing special is happening in nature on that day. The winter solstice happens more than a week before. Christmas, of course, is exactly one week before, and December 25 was celebrated as the beginning of the end of winter in many ancient cultures in the northern hemisphere. But so what? What does that have to do with January 1? My curiosity led me to do a little research.

First, I checked out the whole idea of a New Year celebration. I found out that the oldest one on record took place around 2,000 BC in Babylon, which was in what we now know as Iraq. However, the ancient Babylonians celebrated the New Year in late March because that was the beginning of their new cycle of spring planting. Before the planting, though, they spent eleven days in celebrations of thanksgiving for all the good that the gods had provided the previous year. In a similar way, the ancient Hawaiians celebrated the New Year in November, with four whole months of thanksgiving, feasting, gaming, and getting ready for the next season. In fact, some kind of New Year celebration has been part of virtually every culture on earth as a means of giving thanks for past things of value and making preparations for a year of more blessings to come (hopefully).

Still, why January 1? It isn't a harvest time or a seeding time in either hemisphere. As a point in the orbit of the Earth around the Sun, it doesn't have any particular significance. My research revealed, however, that natural events are not the only things that humans consider significant.

During the early Roman Empire, the first day of the New Year was January 1. Weirdly enough, their January 1 fell on what we now know as March 25, at the beginning of spring. Because various emperors and high-ranking officials placed great value on extending their terms of office, they fiddled with the lengths of months and years until the calendar got so out of whack that Julius Caesar had to put January 1 on its proper date again (March 25) in 46 BC.

Enter the Catholic Church. As the leaders of that body became more politically powerful, they decided to establish their own January 1 in opposition to what they considered a pagan fertility festival. So they created a brand new calendar and made the New Year begin on the Feast of the Circumcision of Jesus, exactly one week after the birth of Christ by their reckoning.

The transition to this new New Year wasn't immediate. From the eleventh to the thirteenth centuries, the Spanish and Portuguese celebrated the New Year on the Catholic January 1, the British celebrated it on March 25, the Italians on December 15 (which was Christmas day at that time), and the French on Easter Sunday. Meanwhile, and still today, the Chinese, Jews, and traditional Hawaiians celebrate New Year based on their own timing. Because the Gregorian calendar is so widely accepted today, some people get to celebrate the New Year twice if they want to.

It's time for a valid question to arise: What is the point of all this?

The point is that people everywhere have always acknowledged in some way the ending of an old cycle and the beginning of a new one. The exact timing of the cycle depends on the value—the importance—that people give to the cycle. As described above, some people may think natural cycles are more important, and others may think religious or political cycles to be so. In addition, people everywhere have decided that the beginning/ending of the cycle is a good time to reflect on what they consider important in their lives, either confirming these values or changing them.

It doesn't matter whether your favorite cycle begins on January 1, your birthday, the spring equinox, the winter solstice, or Boxing Day. There is something inherently and humanly powerful about declaring that one cycle has ended and a new one has begun and then using that transition time to give thanks for value received and to make plans for value to come.

Your values consist of whatever you believe is most important in your life. Your values themselves have value because they govern every aspect of your personal behavior and they influence the behavior of the world around you. In any situation in life, you will always act according to what is most important to you at the time, no matter what the circumstance or what anyone around you says or does. You will always make your decisions based on what you value most. If you are ever surprised by your own behavior, it's because you are not aware of your own values.

As an example, I was discussing values with my adorable wife of more than four decades, and we each discovered something we didn't expect. Though we value our relationship highly, our discussion revealed that we value personal freedom even more. Our relationship has such a high value that we constantly decide to accede to each other's wishes even when that means doing something we don't want to do, or not doing something we do want to do. Since there is so much give and take on both sides, and so much joy in other aspects of the relationship, we consider these restrictions on personal freedom as easily tolerable (although I grumble sometimes just for the heck of it). In other words, the relationship has a higher value than these minor restrictions on our freedom. However, in playing the game of "What if . . . ?" it came out that if these restrictions became "excessive" (by subjective evaluation), then the value of the relationship would diminish accordingly.

The discussion got even more interesting when we discovered that "relationship" and "personal freedom" are very abstract concepts. Behind those abstracts were the things we really valued most: the pleasure of our mutual admiration and respect, and the emotional satisfaction of making our own choices.

Behind all abstract values—love, power, health, freedom, and so on—are the very specific values that move us emotionally and motivate us behaviorally. At any given moment, you will always move toward whatever holds the potential, in your estimation, for the greatest pleasure or the least pain. You cannot avoid making a decision either way because not making a decision is still a decision.

In both California and Hawaii you can almost always tell who the carpenters are: They are the ones with surfboards in their pickup trucks. They bring their boards to work, and when the surf is high enough, the worksite is abandoned. The abstract view is that they value surfing more than working. The specific view is that they think the thrill of riding a big wave is more important than sawing wood for someone else (unless they are in dire need of money to pay the rent). They will usually stay on the job when the surf is mediocre, but when the waves reach a certain height, you know where they can be found.

Another example of values motivating behavior is the person who works so hard "for the family" that he or she ignores the family to the point of isolation and confusion. Here, the abstract value of "family security" is probably based on a very intense personal fear of being criticized for failing to support them. In the pursuit of avoiding criticism, the actual family is lost from view.

The value of the discussion between my wife and myself was that we became more consciously aware of what we value. At the same time, because of our Huna background, we realized that it was all arbitrary. With the flick of a thought, we can change any of our values that we choose to change. We can make important things unimportant and unimportant things important by our will alone. And the value of *that* is that we are more consciously aware of, and careful of, those values we choose to live by.

Deciding to change what you value most in life is an act that has profound consequences for you and those around you because the values you have now also have such consequences. If your life doesn't seem to be working out for you, there might be a problem with your values. If life is working out for you, then it might be a good idea to review what those values are. Any time is a good time to examine what is most important to you, whether to confirm your values or to make some alterations. Therefore, *now* is a good time, too.

Decisions and Persistence

The Hawaiian word *ahonui* is commonly translated as "patience." However, that translation into English can be very misleading, because, as embodied in the word *ahonui*, it doesn't carry quite the same meaning.

Generally, when we talk about patience in English, we mean the ability to suffer hardship, discomfort, or pain without complaint. There is a sense of inner strength or courage about it, but it's essentially a passive concept. Something bad is happening to you, but you put up with it bravely for as long as it takes.

As admirable as that concept might be, it doesn't carry the full meaning of *ahonui*.

Let me tell you one of the stories of Maui that will help to illustrate this. This is a Kauai version, and I'll bring out some of the inner meanings to show the relationship to *ahonui*.

Once a upon a time, long before Captain Cook, Maui
Kupua (who was born on Kauai, of course) was coming

back from O'ahu in his canoe when he thought to himself, "Why are the islands so far apart?" Then he made a decision. "They should all be closer together." After he landed, he went to his mother, Hina, in Wailua and asked for her advice on how to bring this about.

Hina stopped her tapa beating and said, "If you want to bring the islands together, you will have to catch the giant whale, Luehu, with your magic fishhook, Manai-a-ka-lani, and you will have to hold on fast for a long time. If you can do this, Luehu will circle the islands and you will be able to pull them together. Take your brothers with you to help with the canoe, but warn them to always face forward no matter what happens, or you will fail."

So Maui gathered his four brothers, Maui, Maui, Maui, and Maui, and told them what he was going to do. They were excited about such an adventure, and when he warned them about facing forward no matter what, they promised that they would.

At last the canoe, the fishhook, and the brothers were all ready. During a break in the surf, they paddled out into the Kaieiewaho Channel and began their search for the great whale. For days and days they searched, until at last they found Luehu swimming beside Nihoa, the island to the northwest of Kauai. Maui threw his magical fishhook, Luehu caught it in his mouth, and immediately the whale began pulling the canoe through the ocean at high speed.

For many more long days, the Maui brothers held on with determination as the whale pulled them onward. By carefully tugging on the fishing line in just the right way, and by cleverly paddling in just the right way at just the right time, they caused the whale to circle all the islands until one day they found themselves again off the coast of Wailua, facing toward O'ahu.

Luehu was tired now, so while Maui Kupua pulled on the fishing line with all his might, his brothers backpaddled furiously, until slowly, slowly the islands began to pull together. Just then, a canoe bailer, kāliu, floated past the canoe. The eldest Maui, in the steersman position, quickly grabbed it and tossed it behind him in case they should need it.

Unknown to him, the bailer was really a mischievous spirit, an e'epa, who turned into a very beautiful woman. All the people gathered on the shorelines of Kauai and O'ahu exclaimed about her beauty. At first, none of the Maui brothers paid attention, but finally the praises got so loud that Maui's four brothers turned around to see who this beautiful woman was. In that moment, Luehu *felt the weakening of the pull against him and gave one last desperate leap to escape. Without his brothers to help him, Maui Kupua pulled too hard, the fishing line broke,* Luehu *got away, and the islands drifted apart again.*

And we know the story is true because the islands are still far apart today.

Hawaiian legends always contain knowledge hidden below the surface, usually in the form of names that have several meanings. In this story, the hero, Maui Kupua, wants to accomplish a great task, the uniting of the islands, but in order to do this, he has to capture the whale, *Luehu*, with his fishhook, *Manai-a-ka-lani*. Now, *Luehu* means "scattered," and *Manaia-kalani* is "flower lei needle." The scattered islands have to be brought together, perhaps politically, culturally, or socially, like flowers strung on a lei. Where did they find the whale? The old name of the Kauai Channel, *Kaieiewaho*, simply means "The Outer Sea," but it could also refer to the need to go outside of one's normal boundaries. The place where they encountered the whale, Nihoa, was a very sacred place in ancient times. The name means "jagged, sharp," like a row of teeth, and is part of an old saying, *Kū pākū ka pali o Nihoa i ka makani* ("The cliffs of Nihoa stand like a shield against the wind"). This saying refers to someone who faces misfortune with courage.

The most important element in the story is the fishing line. Called *aho*, it also means "breath, to breathe," and "to put forth great effort." Maui must put forth great effort to accomplish his aim, but that still isn't enough. The word *nui* means "big, much, many; something extending over time, or something very important." *Ahonui* means "patience," and it is also the word for "perseverance." This is not the patience of waiting in a line; it is the persistence of knocking on a door until you get an answer. It is not the patience of waiting out a storm; it is the perseverance of moving through a storm to your destination. It is not waiting to get healed; it is doing everything you can to make the healing happen. *Ahonui* can also be translated as "many breaths," the act of moving toward something you want for as many breaths as it takes—the making of the same decisions over and over again.

Hawaiian legends do not always have happy endings because sometimes their purpose is as much to tell you how to succeed as it is to tell you how to fail. In this story, the plan's downfall was caused by *kāliu*, which means "a leaky canoe bailer." *Kā* refers to a canoe bailer, but it is also a strong action word used for tying things together, for making or doing things, and even for fishing. *Liu*, the "leakage," is the leaking away of attention to your purpose, the loss of focus on what is important, the making of decisions that weaken your will. In the story, Maui's brothers, representing aspects of himself, get distracted, and they lose their goal as they lose their focus. Perseverance does not work on a part-time basis.

Fortunately, there are many examples in this world of people who have persevered in the face of seemingly insurmountable odds and who have accomplished more than was thought humanly possible. I have met and talked with a lot of such people, and have read about many more, but one stands out strongly in my memory.

A few years ago I had the privilege of participating in a Hawaii Department of Education program to teach young people about self-esteem, and part of the workshop I gave was incorporated into a video that was distributed in the school system. The best part of the video was not my contribution, however. It was the story of a young girl who became a *hula* dancer. I was mildly impressed when the camera showed her from the waist up, dancing with a group of other girls, all moving gracefully with the same rhythm and gestures. But when the camera pulled back, I was stunned. This lovely young girl was a good dancer, yes, as good as the others. And she had only one leg.

Imagine the patience, the persistence, the suffering, the perseverance, the *ahonui* that this young girl applied to develop the grace and skill that was also difficult for her two-legged sisters. And what gave her this *ahonui*? Where did it come from? How did she maintain her decision to keep going through all the fears and doubts and problems she must have endured? There is only one answer: What gave her the strength of her *ahonui* was the *aloha* she had for the *hula*.

What will give you the strength to persevere in the direction of your dreams and desires, plans and goals, wishes and healings, is the love you have for something that you decide is so important, so valuable, so good that nothing at all can replace it in your mind and in your heart. If your *aloha* is strong enough, you will have the *ahonui* to keep going in spite of doubt, disappointment, fear, misunderstanding, and all the people who tell you that what you want is impossible. In this infinite Universe, the only impossibility is whatever you never attempt, and the only failure is when you decide to give up.

Decisions and Luck

"Luck" is another concept on the list of things that people really don't understand. Most of those who mention it make it sound like a form of predestination. There is a strong tendency to attribute success to "good luck" and failure to "bad luck," as if luck were some sort of grace or curse just dropped on a person by the whimsy of a supernatural being. That being so, it would not matter what decisions you made because the outcome would always be out of your hands. In Huna teaching that is never the case. The sixth principle says that all power comes from within, and that implies free will. Combine the idea of free will with the second principle, that there are no limits, and you come up with the idea that we can make our own luck.

Obviously unconscious luck abounds because a lot of unexpected and unplanned things happen to people. However, remember the teaching that anything we can do unconsciously can also be done consciously, as long as we can figure out *how* to do it. So how can we create or increase our own luck?

A well-known quote gives us one approach. I've been unable to find the original author, but the message is, "Luck is when preparation meets opportunity." The most common interpretation is that the more prepared you are in your field of interest, in terms of skill and knowledge, the more "lucky breaks" you will have in that field. It's probably true, but it doesn't explain the good luck of people who aren't prepared with skill and knowledge. Perhaps there are some other kinds of preparation as well.

I do know that it's quite common for the winners of lotteries to be people who have bought tickets consistently over a long period of time. Perhaps persistence is a factor, but that doesn't explain the luck that happens to people who haven't been persistent in their behavior.

I know that on numerous occasions I have been able to win something in a contest or a raffle by moving into a special kind of mental/emotional state that I can only describe as "casually expectant." It's different than having a charismatic influence, and it's not at all like having a powerful focus. It's more like, "Yeah, it would be really nice to win, and it's OK if I don't. But it would be nice." Emotionally, it's like being passively expectant. It isn't a guaranteed system by any means, but it works more often than not.

It seems to me that good luck happens when you are in harmony with what you want. After considerable thought and practice, I've come up with a process to increase your luck. I call it *ulu pono*, which means "to increase good fortune." Start with a minute on each step, and gradually extend the time you spend in each state. Then practice it in times when you want luck on your side.

1. Imagine what it must feel like to be loved unconditionally by everyone and everything.
2. Imagine what it must feel like to be totally confident and completely free of fear and doubt.
3. Imagine what it must feel like to be lucky all the time.

So, the next time you have an important decision to make, remember what you've learned about values and persistence, and *decide* to be lucky, too.

E pono e! (Good luck!)

12

The Master Formula for Success

O ka pono ke hana'ia a iho mai na lani
Do good until the heavens come down to you
(Blessings come to those who persist in doing good)

In this wrap-up chapter, I'd like to review the ideas we've discussed so far, present new ones, and give you a formula for succeeding at anything.

Why am I giving you another formula for success when so many other authors have done the same thing? Think of it as a chocolate cake recipe: To make a chocolate cake, you basically just mix together flour, water, sugar, eggs, and chocolate; bake them in a pan; and out comes a finished cake. But oh, what a difference between chocolate sponge cake, devil's food cake, and German chocolate cake!

Different writers have put together their own recipes (or formulas), either handed down from generations back or created from their own experience. Formulas, like recipes, allow us to duplicate others' successes, and they give us a framework on which to base our own creative innovations.

In the following pages, I offer a formula for winning with love, based on Huna philosophy, my study of successful people and those who write about success, and my own experiences and observations. It's actually a formula for success of any kind. That is, it is a description of how success happens, no matter who wins or whether or not they realize what they are doing. To continue the metaphor, I want to give you one basic recipe that you can use to make anything you want just by changing the ingredients.

Today we have a society in which millions are homeless and destitute and don't know how to get out of their situation; in which some medical sources report that 70 to 90 percent of illnesses are psychosomatic, leaving people helplessly ill because they don't know how to change their minds; in which more and more businesses are failing and the economy is insecure; and in which divorce rates, domestic violence, and international tensions are steadily on the rise. Powerlessness, which leads to ineffectiveness and despair, is an epidemic.

Naturally, there are things and events that we can't control, but we can always control our response to them. And the more skill we can use in our response, the more influence we have on those things and events even if we can't control them. To switch metaphors, if you are the captain of a sailboat, you can't force the wind and the currents to do what you want. But if you are a skillful captain, you can adjust your sail and your rudder to the wind and the current in order to get where you want to go. It seems logical, then, that if you have a clear and simple strategy for dealing with any conditions you meet, you will always be able to operate at maximum effectiveness. Here, then, is the Master Formula in all its crystal clear simplicity:

$$E = mc^2 - r$$

Look familiar? That's because Albert Einstein used part of it for another purpose a while back. But it means something different here:

*"E" stands for **Effectiveness***
*"m" stands for **motivation***
*"c2" stands for two things: **confidence** and **concentration***
*"r" stands for **resistance***

Written out, the formula says, "Effectiveness equals motivation multiplied by confidence, multiplied again by concentration, and reduced by resistance." To put it even less formally, the way to increase your effectiveness is to increase your motivation, concentration, and confidence, while at the same time eliminating or diminishing the stuff that gets in the way. Let's take a closer look at the various parts of the formula.

Effectiveness

All my life, I've been wandering the face of the earth, seeking the secret of effectiveness. I say all my life in a literal sense because I've been traveling since before I was born. You might object by asking how I could be seeking when I was an embryo or a baby or a young child moving around with my parents, but all of us have been trying to be more effective, consciously or unconsciously, since before conception.

As an egg, we made our way down through our mother's body to where we could be fertilized; and as a sperm, we successfully swam a challenging route to do the fertilizing. As embryos, we organized and multiplied our cells to be effective human beings; and as babies, we immediately began learning and assimilating everything we could in order to effectively survive, grow, and enjoy. It is our essential nature to seek ways of being more effective all the days of our lives. And we do that not only by our own experience but through the experience of others as well.

A long time ago, when I was still very young but on my own, I consciously sought the secret of effectiveness among many traditions, philosophies, and masters. Finally, after crossing oceans and deserts and rivers and mountains over much of the world, I met up with a wise old Hawaiian on top of a volcanic island who told me the secret in a way that I could understand and make use of.

"Life," he said, "is like a bowl of cherries." Before I could groan, he went on to say that first we start with an empty bowl, and then we fill it with cherries. We eat the cherries until the bowl is empty again, then we start filling it again, and that's how life goes on. The empty bowl is us, hungry for experience, and filling the bowl with cherries is gathering experience. Eating the cherries is using or enjoying the experience, which empties the bowl and leaves us hungry for more. Effectiveness has to do with our ability to fill the bowl and use or enjoy the cherries. The more effective we are—that is, the greater our skill—the faster we can fill the bowl, the better the quality of cherries we can fill it with, and the more we can enjoy and use them. However, sometimes in filling the bowl, we put in sticks and leaves and dirt; and sometimes in eating the cherries, we leave the pits in there, too. So even if we are first-class cherry-pickers and skillful cherry-users with well-trained taste buds, the junk and gunk that we collect in our bowl limits our experience until we clean it out again.

We start striving for effectiveness from the time our sperm starts its hazardous journey and our egg picks it out of the lot that's available. We continue as our DNA arranges our cells and orders our growth so we can function as an embryo and a fetus. Once we are born, we start absorbing information like crazy so we can learn how to operate effectively in this strange new world. And as we grow up, the one consistent thing that everyone does is keep on trying to figure out how to cope with, and perhaps even master, ourselves, our relationships, and our environment.

Effectiveness is a universal, powerful, unconscious drive. Adding conscious desires makes it even more powerful. Adding skill, derived from knowledge, experience, and practice, turns it into a potential force for unlimited achievement.

Motivation

Motivation is the urge that moves us into being or doing or having, or into not being or not doing or not having. Every action we undertake, consciously or unconsciously, is in response to an urge of some kind. Our heart beats because of an urge to complete a cycle of tension and relaxation; our hand reaches for a glass of water because of an urge to quench the discomfort of thirst; our mind creates fantasies because of an urge to be doing something different from what we're doing. Life is movement, and movement comes about through a sequence of urges.

Business managers are encouraged to motivate their employees, and teachers are expected to motivate their students—as if motivation were something you could put into another person the way you put gasoline into a car. The practical fact is that all motivation is internal, meaning that it has to come from inside. No one else can actually motivate us. The best anyone else can do—and that's quite a bit for a skilled motivator—is to stimulate and magnify a motivation that already exists in a particular person or group. If you have a motivation to make more money, then a skilled motivator can build on that and get you excited enough to increase your sales, or to sign up for a multi-level marketing plan. But if you are not motivated by a desire for more money, then the same motivator, no matter how skilled, won't be able to budge you to do a thing.

The most powerful motivation—the kind that moves mountains; changes societies; or makes you healthier, wealthier, happier, and more successful—always comes from doing the stimulating and magnifying yourself. The better you understand what it is that motivates you, the easier it will be to motivate yourself.

The most fundamental motivations are toward pleasure and away from pain. Everything you do with your body or your mind, on purpose or out of habit, with conscious or unconscious intent, can be defined as a movement toward pleasure or away from pain—physical, emotional, or mental. There is pleasure in relaxation, so your body seeks rest, your mind seeks diversions, and your spirit may seek solitude on occasion. Yet there is also pleasure in a certain amount of tension, so your body seeks activity, your mind seeks interests, and your spirit may seek out other people. Curiously, you might do exactly the same things in order to move away from pain. Your body may seek rest, your mind diversions, and your spirit solitude because of excessive tension caused by too much activity, conflicting interests, or too many people. On the other hand, pain can also come from insufficient activity, scattered attention, and too much solitude or loneliness. If you want to understand the pleasure/pain idea, it will help you to understand why you do the things you do and why you don't do other things.

Now, you may be thinking that you (or someone else you know) sometimes seem to move toward pain and away from pleasure, and you may wonder how that fits in with what I've just said. Some people persist in painful workouts, others stay in abusive relationships, and still others seem bent on sabotaging themselves at every opportunity. Why is that?

This brings us to a different level of motivation, which is motivation based on love or fear. Because of the fact that we have memory and imagination, we are not limited to pleasure and pain experiences in the present moment. We have the ability to remember pleasure and pain, and we have the ability to anticipate them, or to imagine them happening, in the future. The motivation of love, then, is the urge to re-create a pleasurable experience from the past or to create an imagined pleasurable experience in the immediate or distant future. Of course, I'm making a distinction here between the pleasurable experience of love in the present moment and the motivation of love, which urges us to act in some way.

In a similar fashion, the motivation of fear urges us to avoid a remembered painful experience or an imagined painful experience in the immediate or distant future. And in any given situation, it is the strongest urge—the one that generates the most feeling or the one that we give the most importance to—that determines our final action.

So a person who persists in painful workouts may do it because he or she is more afraid of a remembered painful experience of being fat, or because of a real love for a fit and healthy body (or some combination of the two); a person who stays in an abusive relationship may do so because of a greater fear of being alone, or because of a love for the imagined potential in the other person; and a self-saboteur may fear remembered criticism for any past accomplishment, may fear imagined consequences of success, or may even be striving for success to please someone else while they actually have more love for meditating on an mountain.

Fear and love each generate two different responses. Fight and flight, which you may remember from introductory psychology classes, are fear responses. In any situation in which fear is the prime motivator, you may react by trying to get away from the situation; or you may react by trying to get rid of it, depending on the situation and your own state of mind and habit. If a bull is chasing you, you would probably do your best to get out of its way, but if you are Conan the Barbarian or Xena, you might stand there and try to beat it senseless.

The two love responses are peace and play. Using the bull again, if love is the prime motivator (say you really love animals), you might adopt a behavior pattern designed to calm and soothe the beast so you can pet and comfort it. Or, if you are a toreador or an ancient Cretan athlete, you might just play with the bull until you are both tired out.

While love and fear are pretty basic extensions of pleasure and pain, you can already see that individual motivations can be rather complex. For instance, why do we eat? Fundamentally, we eat because eating is pleasurable and not eating is painful, and because we love some effects of eating and/or fear some effects of not eating. But this still doesn't tell you much about the more specific motivations for eating that may change from person to person and from time to time. On various occasions, I have eaten because I was hungry, because I enjoyed the company, because I wanted to try a new food, and because I wanted to be polite, to name a few reasons. Some of these reasons were based on desires, which are things we want that motivate us, and some of them were based on needs, which are things we think we have to have to motivate us. Let's look at different types of needs to understand the complexities of individual motivations.

Felt Needs

I learned about felt needs when I was in West Africa working in community development, and I found that the concept applies to groups of any kind as well as to individuals. A felt need is the particular conscious or semiconscious motivation of the moment that urges a group or an individual to take action. It is called the felt need in contrast to the obvious need.

As an example, one African village I visited had several obvious needs: improved sanitation, more water, better nutrition, and others, which the local government and international agencies had unsuccessfully tried to meet. Public latrines were installed, but they were seldom used because no one had wanted them in the first place; a new pump was put on the well, but it was abandoned when it broke because it was the government's pump; and nutrition classes were ignored because the new recommended foods tasted strange and were not readily available.

In spite of this unpromising past history, I got the chief to call a village meeting, where I asked them if there were any way in which they wanted to improve their village. This caused a lot of consternation because no one had ever asked them what they wanted before. After several hours of animated discussion, they told me that they wanted to repair the chief's hut because its present state of disrepair was a disgrace to the village. Had I been a government official, I would have gotten angry and told them all the more important things they needed. But since I was a free agent, I could listen to their felt need—the need that they really *felt* was important.

To shorten the story, I helped them to repair the chief's hut, making sure that they retained a proprietary pride by doing most of the work and supplying most of the materials themselves. At the next village meeting, they expressed a desire to clean up the center of the village, and so we did that. We went on from there to build family latrines for convenience and prestige, start market gardens for an extra cash crop, buy a new pump with family contributions to water the gardens, improve nutrition by sharing recipes, and even start an officially recognized credit union by building on and expanding a traditional form of putting money aside for emergencies. In sum, I helped the villagers to accomplish everything that the government wanted and more by working with what the people felt they wanted rather than what someone else told them they should want. They did the same things but for different reasons.

The felt needs of individuals can be quite different from their obvious needs, yet the obvious needs can be addressed by satisfying the felt needs effectively. When I used to do personal counseling, I found that the concept of health was a meaningless abstraction for most people. In other words, it was not an effective motivator for changing habits. People lost weight so they would look good or so they would fit into certain kinds of clothes; they stopped smoking so they would smell better, or to avoid criticism from friends and family; they engaged in self-healing practices because they were afraid of helplessness or the pain of orthodox treatment, or because illness was getting in the way of play or work. There may be someone out there for whom health itself is a felt need, but I have never met such a person. Nevertheless, all the people I helped became healthier when their felt needs were met.

Since felt needs are not obvious, it's possible that we might not even be fully aware of what our own felt needs are. The more we are conscious of them, however, the more we can use them to modify our behavior in ways that will greatly increase our chances for success. To assist you in recognizing your own felt needs, here is a list of the seven most common types:

Awareness (Includes Curiosity, the Desire for Knowledge, and the Desire for Security)
Even cows have curiosity, so this is a part of our animal heritage. Once, while on a boring bus trip to the airport, a man took his suitcase down from a rack to open it. I noticed that the rest

of us were watching him as if he were doing the most fascinating thing in the world. In humans, though, curiosity can expand into a felt need for news, gossip, soap operas, and a love of wandering just to see what's over the next hill. Maybe you are one of those people, or you know of one, who can't eat breakfast without a newspaper or can't wait for the next bridge game to hear what's happening in the neighborhood.

The desire for knowledge may have a practical relationship to your vocation or hobby, but it might also be an advanced form of curiosity. A lot of people, like me, have a felt need for increasing our knowledge of the world around us whether it is practical or not. Many research scientists have it, as do the people who read encyclopedias and almanacs for fun. Approaching it from a different point of view, a felt need for security can drive people to increase their awareness of the world in order to avoid unpleasant surprises. It's possible for this to turn into obsessive paranoia, but I know of at least one person who has used it to develop a very fine system of personality analysis, so she knows ahead of time how to deal with the various people she meets.

Freedom (Includes the **Need to Relax,** the **Desire to Be Free of Restraint,** the **Desire to Express Your Own Will,** and the **Desire to Move and to Explore**)
The felt need to relax is very different from the obvious need to relax. I've known people who looked like perfect pictures of relaxation but still wanted to relax more, and I've known people who were clearly as tight as a drum but didn't even realize they were tense.

The felt urge for freedom from restraint can refer to physical restraint, of course, like adults in prison or children in school, but some people feel unduly restrained by marriage, friendship, working conditions, or society's regulations. And still others feel mentally restrained by the social or professional limitations put on their vocation.

A felt need for self-determination can be a national issue in a colony or a country bound economically and politically to another against its will. Or it can be a personal issue for someone who feels bound economically or emotionally to another person.

The desire to move and explore can be akin to the desire for more awareness, but not necessarily. A woman in one of my courses in England sat quietly through the discussion and mental exercises of the first morning, and then she said to me, "Thank you very much. It's a good course, but I'm leaving because I need more body movement."

Also, as I know from traveling to various areas around the world, there are some who have a strong felt need just to move along the open road, the open trail, or the open sea under the wide open sky whether anything new is learned or not.

Purpose (Includes the Desire for Meaning, Guidelines, and Self-Justification by Serving a Cause Larger Than Yourself)

This felt need is so prevalent that there are a multitude of jokes and stories about people who wander far and long to find a wise old teacher who can tell them the meaning of life. Psychics, prophets, psychiatrists, and therapists of many kinds make a living helping people to discover meaning and purpose in the events of their lives. (Some of my students think me old but not too wise when I suggest to them that *we* ourselves give life and events their meaning, and *we* create our purpose.)

The felt need for guidelines starts when we are children trying to figure out the rules for coping in this world, and it continues for the rest of our lives even if we only want to know which rules to break. And if it were not for the felt need to serve a cause, then religions, charities, political parties, and social/environmental action groups would be in very bad shape indeed.

Sensation (Includes **All Desire for Pleasurable Stimuli,** such as **Beautiful Sights and Sounds, Delicious Tastes, Touching, Sex, Excitement, Movement,** and **Dance)**
Art and music would not exist were it not for the felt need of artists to create and the felt need of many others to enjoy their creations. Just think for a moment on how much motivation it takes to create and support art museums and galleries, symphony orchestras, rock concerts, and the movie and recording industries. Great chefs can only be great when there are those with the desire to appreciate their cuisine, and great restaurants have to do more than just serve nutritious food.

While touching and being touched is a powerful and beneficial experience, it is not always a felt need except among people from certain cultural groups (like the Italian side of my family) and among those who enjoy such physical interactions as contact sports, massage, and contact dancing.

Sex, naturally, in all its various aspects, is the primo sensory experience for most people, but when it is not available then excitement of any kind is better than no sensation at all.

Excitement becomes more important to people when other emotional outlets are either closed off or unsatisfactory, which may help to explain the apparent felt needs for horror movies and novels and the magnetic attraction of fires, disasters, and life-threatening sports.

There is no question that movement is a felt need with most children, particularly my three-year-old granddaughter, and dance, whether classical, free-form, or aerobic, has many needful devotees.

Relating (Includes the Desire to Be Accepted, Acknowledged, or Recognized by Other People, the Desire for Friendship and Intimacy, and the Desire to Belong to a Greater Whole)

After air and food, I'd say the most basic felt need for human beings is acceptance—by their peers, by those whom they admire or hold in authority, or by themselves. People will even give up sex for acceptance much more readily than they will give up acceptance for sex. In many cultures the worst conceivable punishment is banishment, exile, ostracism, or solitary confinement. More specifically, painters and sculptors need benefactors and actors, and comedians need audiences. Actors dread an empty theatre, but they dread critical reviews even more. Comedians, and other performers who interact with an audience, may become obsessed with the unresponsiveness of a single individual even if they have received abundant praise from everyone else. As a public speaker, this was a problem I had to do a lot of work on. If all eyes weren't on me all the time, I thought I was being ineffective. Finally, and fortunately for my ego, I discovered that different people have different ways of listening, so now I'm comfortable at the podium even when people look away, have their eyes closed, or lie down on the floor and apparently go to sleep.

Business and political leaders know that titles and public recognition are often effective substitutes for higher salaries. Honoring people is one of our most important social rituals because there is such a widespread felt need for it both among the honorees and those doing the honoring.

Friendship is a strong felt need. Because of cultural values and training, the felt need for intimacy in a relationship at the present time seems to be more prevalent among the female portion of our population, but the increasingly popular "men's movement" is showing that many men have felt the need but have skillfully kept it hidden because of the need for peer and social acceptance This demonstrates that one felt need can suppress another, depending on which is stronger at the moment. For some people the felt need is for a transpersonal relationship, a connection with a greater whole which could be, according to individual desires, a special relationship with nature, with the earth, or with God as that individual understands it.

Power (Includes the Desire for Strength, Ability, Talent, Skill, Influence, Money, and Control)

The urge for power in some form is perfectly natural. Without it we would never learn to walk or talk or do and improve the myriad of things that we take for granted as part of living, from such simple activities as cashing a check and driving a car to more complex ones involved in carrying out a profession. It is always there as an underlying felt need in everything we undertake.

But for some people the need becomes so strong that it takes them far beyond the ordinary. They don't just want to lift chairs, they want to lift cars. They aren't content with acting, they want to direct. It isn't enough for them to be president of a company; they want to lead a nation. And there are those for whom taking charge of their own lives is not satisfying enough—they want to control the lives of others as well.

Although the urge for power might have its roots in fear or in the desire for acceptance or recognition, the felt need may also be for power itself—the heady sense of being in charge of destiny. A politician can feel it, a gambler can feel it, and so can leaders, artists, athletes, mystics, and many others. And though any felt need can become an obsession when fear is the hidden driver, an obsession with power can affect so many others in a negative way. Abuses of power occur so often that a lot of people are afraid of the power concept entirely. They not only avoid it as much as possible, but they may even revile others who have it. They may even give the responsibility of their personal power to someone else.

Whenever the issue of power comes up there is almost always someone who has the felt need to repeat Lord Acton's aphorism, which I quoted before: "Power corrupts, and absolute power corrupts absolutely." This serves to reinforce the fear of power, but the phrase is nonsense. Power itself does not corrupt. The corruption only occurs when power is combined with one or more of the Great Separators: fear, hatred, or indifference. When power is combined with love, however, there is nothing better. As Britain's great Edmund Burke put it: "I know of nothing sublime which is not some modification of power."

One form of power that most people in modern society perceive as a felt need is money. It gives us the power to purchase desired goods and services, and it enables us to influence the world around us in many ways. Even though people have many reasons for feeling a need for money, such as security, acceptance, and freedom, the need for money itself is because of the power it supposedly has to fill those other needs. There is at least some truth in this bumper sticker saying: "People who say that money can't buy happiness just don't know where to shop."

Achievement (Includes the Desire to Reach Goals, Win Competitions, Break Records, Right Wrongs, Fix What Isn't Working, Heal Others, and Help People to Be More Effective)

I was very impressed with the felt need for personal or vicarious achievement when I visited the giant soccer stadium at Maracana in Rio de Janeiro, which seats 200,000 people. And that's only one symbol among thousands, including the

Olympics and the Super Bowl, that express the incredible amounts of time, energy, and money that go into sporting events around the world. The felt need is often as strong or stronger among the people watching the events as it is among the participants. And don't forget the Oscars, Emmys, Grammys, and other performance awards that motivate and fascinate so many people as well.

Many of us have our own personal achievement agendas that don't get publicized but move us just as strongly. And in spite of controversy about them, much social good has been accomplished by people with felt needs to right wrongs in such organizations as the ACLU, Amnesty International, and the Sierra Club. Let's be thankful, too, for the hundreds of thousands of professionals and nonprofessionals who express their urge to heal and help.

Did any of the felt needs we've just discussed resonate with you? If not, take some time to explore your own felt needs. Clearly defining them will give you a better sense of what motivates you—an important component of the success formula.

Confidence

Confidence is the wonderful feeling of certainty that you have the resources—the time, energy, ability, strength, support, and so on—to do what you want to do. It is also the similar feeling of certainty that something you want to happen is going to happen. Confidence can be externally or internally based, and while an increase in either one will increase effectiveness, it is the second kind that has the greatest potential.

External confidence comes from believing that you can count on the consistent behavior of someone or something outside of yourself. This kind of confidence is based on memories of the past, experience in the present, and expectations about the future—highly influenced by your belief in someone else's authority. So we believe that the seasons will roll on as they always have because that's the way it's been for as long as we can remember, we can observe part of the sequence right now, and we are already making plans for the rest of this year or longer. Besides, our parents, teachers, and authors of books have told us over and over again that that's the way it is. However, if we decide to believe in the prophecies of doomsayers we can discard all of that knowledge and experience and confidently expect the earth to turn over any day now, leaving us (of course) and a few chosen others to start rebuilding the world the way we want it. The main problem with externally based confidence is that it is entirely dependent on events, circumstances, and decisions over which we have no control and limited influence.

Internally based confidence comes from your decisions about yourself—from beliefs about your worth, skills, ability to cope with change, and source of power. The best way to increase internal confidence is to make two decisions: first, to decide that what you want to believe is true; and second, to decide never to doubt the first decision.

Confidence increases effectiveness by (1) reducing the inhibiting effect that fear has on your skills and abilities, and (2) stimulating you to be alert for opportunities. This is about the place where a couple of questions usually arise in some people's minds. Even though I have already mentioned them, here they are again as reminders.

"What about being overconfident?" some people will ask. I don't think there is such a thing. What people call overconfidence is really arrogance masking fear. Others will ask, "What about expecting too much and being disappointed?" Well, disappointment is really the experience of feeling bad because something didn't turn out the way you wanted it to. So one solution is to expect everything to turn out badly and then maybe be pleasantly surprised by something good once in a while. However, that's a pretty unhappy way to live, and it's too easy to get into the habit of making even good things look bad when they happen. Another solution is to train yourself not to have any expectations, but that turns into not having any purpose, goals, or plans, which might be all right for a beach bum or a mystic but not for you and me. A more useful approach is to go ahead and have your great expectations as you acknowledge that not having everything always turn out the way you want it is just one of the hazards of living.

Like motivation, confidence is one of the necessary ingredients in the recipe for effectiveness.

Concentration

Concentration is what keeps our physical, emotional, and mental energy moving in one direction long enough to produce effects. The longer the concentration lasts, the stronger the effects. Without enough concentration, you never work long enough to finish a job or play long enough to finish a game; you don't sustain a desire long enough to carry you through the rough spots; and you don't think long enough to solve a problem or develop a new idea. What we call a lack of concentration is either a series of short bursts of concentration on different things or extended concentration on something other than what we or others think we should be concentrating on.

Sometimes, when I walk into my office, I am overwhelmed by all the things that are competing for my attention, and if I keep shifting my attention from one thing to another, I don't get much done. One technique I use to help my concentration is to heap everything in one big pile and then start working through it one piece of paper at a time. On the other hand, when my children were growing up, they were very good at extended concentration on games or television when I thought they should be concentrating on chores or homework. To be fair, my wife has learned that when I'm reading a novel, she had better not assume that any response I've made to her means that I actually heard her.

Concentration can be easy or hard, depending on whether it is natural or forced. Natural concentration occurs when you are involved in something that you believe is enjoyable, interesting, or important—any activities that are currently satisfying your felt needs of being, doing, or having. If you like sports a lot, then it's easy to concentrate on watching or playing a game. If your hobby is raising horses, then it's easy to read a book or listen to a lecture on their care and training.

Forced concentration is what you have to use when what you are doing is not particularly enjoyable, interesting, or important to you, but you still have to do it. A lot of children put homework into this category, as a lot of adults do for the preparation of tax returns. But since no action is ever taken without some kind of motivation, forced concentration is only effective if it has the promise or expectation of some kind of reward or punishment beyond the task at hand. And reward—the promise of pleasure, benefit, or satisfaction of some felt need—always brings out better effort than the fear of punishment. People will do the least they can to minimize punishment and the most they can to maximize reward. If you have to do something because you'll get punished if you don't, it isn't likely that you will put out your best effort.

Let's say you're a teenager, and you've been told to clean your room or you won't get your allowance. It wouldn't be surprising if all you did was throw a bedspread over your bed and press it down a little so it would look like it was made, put your clothes into one pile, and toss most of the junkier stuff into your closet. But if you were told to clean your room because the neighbors were coming over for a tour of the house and they were bringing their own groovy teenager of the opposite sex with them, it would also not be surprising if you vacuumed, scrubbed, folded, polished, wiped, and straightened until your room was worthy of *Better Homes and Gardens*.

Therefore, the best way to increase concentration is to make the object of your concentration more enjoyable, interesting, or important; or to make the reward for doing it more effective in satisfying a felt need. Concentrating on learning how to play the piano is easy if you love making music; concentrating on a chess game is easy if you are fascinated by strategy; concentrating on what a teacher has to say is easy if you value the information; and concentrating on making money is easy if you really, really want to go to Hawaii.

Resistance

In the master formula for success, resistance must be subtracted from the other contributing factors. Every change also produces a resistance to that change. It seems like the law of inertia—that an object at rest tends to resist being moved, while an object in movement tends to resist being stopped or moved in a different direction—applies not only in the realm of classical physics but in the areas of physical, emotional, and mental behavior as well.

To put it another way, existing habits tend to maintain themselves. This is great and extremely useful as long as the habits are beneficial. It's a good thing that our heart and lungs keep up the habits of beating and breathing and that our habits of language and coping skills are maintained from day to day. But if the beating of our heart is too fast, the breathing of our lungs too shallow, our language inappropriate, and our coping skills inadequate, then change is in order even if it isn't easy. If we can find some way to reduce resistance, however, then change, in the form of a movement toward greater effectiveness, will be easier.

There are four main factors operating in our lives that reduce our happiness by causing resistance to increases in motivation, concentration, and confidence—the key factors of success. The resistance factors are Fear, Unhappiness, Doubt, and Stress. Forming an acronym from the first letter of each, I call them the FUDS, and they can operate individually or in combination. Let me explain:

Fear (including anxiety, panic, and terror) reduces motivation by directing our energies away from something rather than toward it. Specifically, it narrows awareness, restricts freedom, makes us hesitate to carry out a purpose, inhibits relationships, drains away power, and frustrates achievement. In addition, it reduces concentration by diverting attention, and it reduces confidence by creating negative expectations.

Unnatural fear—not the instinctual kind that warns us of immediate danger but the manufactured kind, based on memory and fantasy—is something we can well do without. The antidote for fear is simply hope—just good, old-fashioned, positive expectation. A number of people have put down hope in recent years, terming it pollyannaish, unrealistic, and a sop for weakminded souls. But hope has been the companion of humanity's greatest men and women, and no one has ever achieved greatness without it. For all the dangers and delusions that it may promote, no one has described its practical benefit more succinctly than eighteenth-century English thinker Samuel Johnson: "Where there is no hope, there is no endeavor."

As fear is rooted in memory and fantasy, so is hope. In fear we select pain and failure out of the memory storehouse and project them forward into a fantasized future. In hope we use the same process to select pleasure and success from memories and project them forward into a different fantasized future. It's useful to consider that any thoughts we have about the future are only fantasies until the fantasy becomes a present reality, with or without our help. Put in practical terms: As long as your expectations about the future are fantasies anyway, why not make them good ones?

Unhappiness (including anger, resentment, guilt, sadness, sorrow, and grief) is the worst plague that besets the modern world. Individually, it probably causes more illness than any other single factor; socially, it destroys people, communities, and nations. When combined with fear, it wreaks the most terrible havoc imaginable in every aspect of life.

In seminars, students will often question me about the benefits of unhappiness, since even unhappy habits must have a benefit to continue their existence. Well, anger can motivate you out of apathy and help you to overcome fear. Resentment can give you a false but satisfying sense of power or control over someone else. Guilt can induce us to change our ways for the better. Sadness can sometimes have a strangely pleasurable, bittersweet quality to it. Sorrow can give birth to compassion. And grief can be a way of honoring a beloved or admired person who has passed on. I don't have any problem with the positive benefits that unhappiness can produce in the short term. But extended unhappiness always works against the best interests of individuals and society because it is essentially a negation of happiness. Unrestrained and undisciplined, anger leads to destructive violence, resentment leads to illness and/or vengeance, guilt leads to illness and self-destruction, sadness leads to apathy, sorrow leads to despair, and grief leads to futility.

You might think that the antidote for unhappiness is happiness, but that's too big a jump for most people. The most effective antidote is really forgiveness. Since unhappiness comes from resisting what was, what is, or what you imagine will be, forgiveness of someone or something for not being or doing what you want will decrease resistance, diminish unhappiness, and cause happiness to rise up naturally.

Doubt (including negative judgment, criticism, and skepticism) is said to be our best friend and worst enemy all in one. It is our best friend when it causes us to exercise discretion in our actions, to analyze our plans, and to question external authority. It is our worst enemy when it limits our focus to what is wrong, makes us negate anything positive, and creates the habit of always questioning internal authority.

It is said that once, when Satan was showing a guest around a museum deep in his hellish domain and they walked past dazzling displays of the Great Temptor's best weapons in his war against goodness (Greed, Avarice, Jealousy, and Hate), his guest noticed a small case set off by itself and containing nothing but an old, worn and pitted wedge. When asked about it, Satan laughed and said, "Oh, that! That's my best weapon of all, for I know I can always count on it when everything else fails. That's Doubt."

Doubt is a real destroyer of effectiveness when it becomes habitual, judging everything in a negative way with no acknowledgment given to the positive side. In the form of criticism, it can deflate motivation faster than anything else. An unfortunate misapprehension in our society is the terrible idea that criticism makes people better. This results in children, as well as adults, being constantly told what's wrong with their behavior, their looks, their thoughts, and everything about them. Why can't Johnny read? Probably because he was criticized so much for being slow and making mistakes that he just quit trying. Why does Jane have low self-esteem? Very likely it's because her mother, father, sister, brother, teacher, employer, and friends all tried to "help" her by telling her what was wrong with her, and she lost her self-respect.

The theory behind the practice of emphasizing mistakes, or behavior that doesn't conform to the rules, is that once a person realizes that what they are doing is "wrong," they will be motivated to correct themselves and do it "right." In real life it seldom works out because the right behavior is rarely acknowledged or praised. Unless someone has a powerful internal felt need to accomplish something, constant criticism without any emotional rewards turns motivation into vapor. And if someone under heavy criticism does accomplish something worthwhile, it's in spite of the criticism and not because of it. Doubt as criticism also breaks concentration, making learning more difficult because the person is more worried about making mistakes than in developing skill. One of my students, attending a course on Kauai, spent her spare time taking tennis lessons. For a while she endured the instructor's tendency to dwell on her errors, and then, because of what she was learning in the course, she asked the tennis instructor point blank to start complimenting her on what she did right. The surprised instructor did it awkwardly at first, but when her game improved rapidly, he ended up dropping nearly all the criticisms and reinforced all her good points. She ended up learning faster than anyone he had taught before.

Confidence, naturally, is also dissipated by doubt, particularly self-doubt. When Arnold Schwarzenegger was competing for the Mr. Universe weightlifting title, I remember him saying something to the effect that he never allowed the slightest negative thought to enter his head during preparation or competition because even the smallest doubt could cause him to lose his edge.

Like everything else, doubt has its positive aspects. It's good to have discernment to tell whether something is good, valuable, or worthwhile. Critical analysis, a highly developed skill, is a very useful adjunct to effectiveness, especially when combined with positive reinforcement, but most of what tries to pass for critical analysis is no more than negative reinforcement. Healthy skepticism is necessary in a world where con artists of every imaginable type, in every imaginable field of human endeavor, are running rampant, but the kind of skepticism that refuses to consider any beneficial potential is not healthy at all.

Stress (including any form of tension caused by physical, emotional, and mental stress) has become more familiar to us through studies linking it to health, social, and learning problems. The emphasis here is on excessive stress because the only totally stress-free state is called dead. We need stress to live and grow, but too much of it gets in the way of this process.

Excessive stress, resulting in excessive tension, comes from excessive resistance to people, events, and circumstances. Most people think that stress comes from the outside—that it's someone else's fault or that it's caused by circumstances. The reality is that all of our stress comes from ourselves. People and events produce conditions that we have to deal with. Stress occurs only to the extent that we resist those conditions. If someone gets angry at me and I don't care, I won't be stressed. But if I'm upset or reactive to the anger, I'll tense up physically, mentally, and emotionally. Stress comes from an internal reaction that causes tension of all kinds and reduces effectiveness when it becomes excessive.

The Feedback Factor

Of course, there is constant feedback between all parts of the formula, just as in mathematics. One way I've already mentioned—that effectiveness increases as motivation, confidence, and concentration increase and resistance decreases.

However, it is also true that motivation, confidence, and concentration increase and resistance decreases as our effectiveness increases. In other words, succeeding encourages the very factors that bring about success while discouraging the factors against it. So by acknowledging all your wins or successes, no matter how small, you support your ability to succeed more often.

In addition, whenever you increase your motivation, you help increase your confidence and concentration; as you build your confidence, your motivation and concentration increase; and as you develop your skill of concentration, motivation and confidence increase as well. And all the while the FUDS get weaker and weaker. This is the way to success.

In describing the Master Formula and the elements that make it up, I have had to use a lot of words. After reading about it, however, all you have to do is print out or write the formula on the back of a business card or small piece of paper and set it where you can look at it once in a while. Once you know the formula, putting it into practice becomes simply a matter of discipline and dedication. If you reflect on it occasionally, I think you'll be surprised at how much of the formula, and the wisdom of Huna, comes back to you in times of need.

And now you know something about *Ka Huna*, the ancient wisdom or secret of turning inner knowledge into outer success. I hope that throughout the book you've come to see that Huna is not a set of techniques or a list of rules but a way of perceiving the world. Once you embrace the spirit of Huna, embodied in its seven principles, your whole outlook changes, your love and power increase, and life becomes an adventure filled with joy and harmony.

I'm going to end with a quote from a man who lived a life filled with the *aloha* spirit. Although not a Hawaiian, he loved the islands and visited many times.

*"I've always been in the right place at the right time. Of course,
I steered myself there."*

—Bob Hope

Hawaiian Cultural Figures

Kamehameha the Great (ca. 1758–1819)

King of the Hawaiian Islands

Kamehameha the Great conquered the Hawaiian Islands and established the Kingdom of Hawaii. Known for his great ambition and devotion to Hawaiian culture, he united the Hawaiian Islands into a single kingdom recognized by all the major world powers of his time. He embodied all seven of the Huna principles in his practice and promotion of awareness, freedom, focus, presence, love, power, and harmony.

King Kalākaua (1836–1891)

The Last King of Hawaii

King Kalākaua is known for being the first monarch in history to circumnavigate the globe. He did so and met with numerous heads of state in an attempt to learn from other world leaders and improve foreign relations. King Kalākaua had a lasting impact on Hawaiian culture, due in large part to his support of Hawaiian legends, *hula*, music, healing, and the preservation of esoteric knowledge.

Duke Kahanamoku (1890–1968)

Surfing Pioneer and Olympic Swimmer

Hawaiian legend Duke Kahanamoku won three gold and two silver medals for swimming in the Olympics of 1912, 1920, and 1924; introduced surfing as a sport to the world; became the first person to be inducted into the Swimming Hall of Fame and the Surfing Hall of Fame; and served thirteen consecutive terms as sheriff of Honolulu. His passion for surfing, the ocean, and swimming has made him a beloved figure in Hawaiian history.

Ka'ahumanu (1768–1832)
The Favorite Wife of Kamehameha the Great

Ka'ahumanu was the youngest and favorite wife of Kamehameha the Great, and she encouraged him in his efforts to unify the Hawaiian Islands. When the old king died, she announced to the kingdom that the king's dying wish was to name her as Queen Regent to the throne (something like a prime minister). Such was her presence that she maintained her control of the kingdom with no opposition from 1819 to 1832 and even named Kinau, a daughter of another wife of Kamehameha I, as her successor. As a champion of women's rights and a firm proponent of Hawaiian unity, she embodied *mana*, or personal power.

Lili'uokalani (1838–1917)
The Last Queen of Hawaii

It was immense love of the Hawaiian Islands and its people that caused the last queen of Hawaii, Lili'uokalani, to abdicate her throne under protest, rather than allow the shedding of blood, when an armed force, backed by the U.S. military, took over the government in 1893. She recorded her own views of the government overthrow, thus becoming the first female Native Hawaiian author. She is remembered for her spirit of *aloha*, expressed in her actions on behalf of the Hawaiian people, and for her love songs, of which the famous *Aloha 'Oe* is still sung today at thousands of gatherings.

Glossary

ahonui: Patience, perseverance.

aloha: Love, compassion, kindness, affection; to be happy with someone or something and to share this happiness.

Haipule: "A prayer, blessing, or spell"; a process for organizing and strengthening one's thoughts, feelings, and behaviors based on the simple theory that by changing yourself you can change your experience.

heiau: One of the ancient Hawaiian temples.

Ho'olapa-i-ka-hā: "To animate the breath" or "to spread life"; a simple yet powerful breath-energizing technique used to build awareness of energy and energy amplification.

ho'omanamana: "Empowerment"; also the name of a Hawaiian empowerment technique.

ho'opua'i-waho-ka-mana: "Cause the mana to flow outward"; also known as the Radiation Technique, an energy-moving exercise designed to direct the mind, to invite imagination.

Huna: "Secret"; Hawaiian esoteric knowledge dating back to ancient times.

i 'ano: "Being here"; also a Hawaiian technique or exercise for getting one fully centered in the present moment.

'ike: "To see, know, feel, perceive, be aware, understand"; in its active form of *ho'ike*, it means "to show, demonstrate, explain, reveal, experience."

kahuna: A recognized expert in a certain field related to Hawaiian culture.

kala: "To loosen, untie, free, release, forgive"; often associated with the philosophy that all limits are arbitrary and the Universe itself is infinite.

kalakupua, or kupua: Similar to *shamanism*.

kala mana: The power of releasing energy.

Kanehunamoku: "The hidden island of Kane," a famous spirit island of Hawaiian legend; in many tales, humans travel here to learn esoteric knowledge and then return to share that knowledge with the rest of humanity.

kapa: A bark cloth utilized in the construction of the ancient heiau, or temples, of Hawaii; it was partially draped over the wooden temple framework called *'anu'u*.

ka'u: Fear, meaning "to hold back," as in the holding back of energy.

ka'uka'u: Inhibiting energy as the result of fear.

kaunu: "Positive passion" or "to make passionate love"; used when viewing love on practical terms, as one would when one has a passionate interest in something.

konane: A Hawaiian game similar to checkers.

Ku: The subconscious, or "body mind."

kumu hula: A *hula* master.

ku'upau: "Uninhibited flow"; its meaning also includes bringing an end to complexes and entanglements, releasing and letting things flow in a different way.

lualike: With *lua* meaning "to duplicate" and *like* meaning "to be like, to resemble," this compound is known as the Duplication Effect, a useful power/energy ability of the body and mind.

makakū: "The creative imagination of an artist"; by its roots, *maka* and *ku*, it could also mean "fixed eyes" or "view that resembles something else." As a technique, it means to imagine what you want.

mākia: "Aim, purpose; to aim or strive for; to concentrate on"; this concept goes along with the idea that one can have/do whatever one wishes if the proper energy and attention is directed toward realizing that goal.

Mākia mana: "The power of focus"; it is through this truth/belief that the third principle of Huna is possible: "Energy flows where attention goes."

mamake: One of numerous Hawaiian words meaning "desire," this form references the kind of desire that increases energy tremendously and influences change in your life or in the world around you.

mana: "Supernatural or divine power, miraculous power, authority, power," which one finds—like all of creation—within oneself.

manawa: Related to time, its roots, *mana* and *wa*, can be translated as "time of power"; a second meaning is "affections, feelings, emotions," which dwell only in the present moment; and a third meaning is "anterior fontanel," the place on top of the head where the skull bones come together; symbolically, this is the connection to spirit, in the now.

pāhola: "Dissipation," which is the exact opposite of concentration, or focused energy.

paniolo: A Hawaiian cowboy.

pono: A concept of goodness, rightness, or appropriateness.

tapa: A type of cloth made from tree bark that was used for clothing, blankets, wrapping, candle wicks, and caulking the seams in boats and ships, among other things.

ulu pono: "To increase good fortune"; also the name of a process in which one uses imagination to visualize luck and thereby bring more good fortune into one's life.